THE BIGGEST ISSUE?

SUE SMITH with IAN RAYNER

THE BIGGEST ISSUE?

A powerful story
of pain, addiction
and ultimate
freedom.

British Library Cataloguing in Publication Data

A catalogue record for this book is available from the British Library.

ISBN 0-9545006-0-1

Design by 4-9-0 ltd.
Cover photograph by Marc Whitford.
Typeset by Kirsten Barber.
Printed in Great Britain by Biddles Limited, Guildford, Surrey.

Sue Smith is the author of *'Romanian Rescue'*, *'Power to Parent'* and *'God's Fingerprint'* (all Hodder & Stoughton).

She is married with five sons and lives near York.

ACKNOWLEDGEMENTS

Sometimes thank you doesn't seem to be a big enough word but, from the bottom of my heart, I wish to thank the following people, not only for helping in the writing of this book, but also for putting up with me during the process, as it proved to be a more emotional experience than I had first anticipated.

For the production of this book my thanks must go to my good friend Matthew Wadsworth who bore the brunt of my emotions more than most during the writing of the original draft – for his time and effort in what often seemed too big a task I am very grateful; to Sue Smith for the great sacrifice she has made, despite being a mother to five boys, a wife to Graham, teaching two days a week and running two holiday cottages – a mammoth effort in writing and adding flesh to the bones; to Kirsten Barber who has proofread and typeset this book – no small task; to Paul Airy for the wonderful cover and for all his technical expertise; and to Marcus Whitford for his professionalism while doing the photography. (They say don't work with children and animals, well he certainly had his hands full with me and Ziggy!)

Thanks also to Glyn and Ruth for their belief in me and for all their support, and to their son Joshua who has helped me keep life in perspective throughout some difficult times during this venture – I couldn't have done it without you; to my two adopted aunties, Andrea and Sue, who work in the office, for the time they have gladly given whenever it has been needed; to all the people of the Isle of Man who have helped and supported me, particularly my family with whom I have enjoyed renewed and restored relationships; and to Molly and the people of Leeds.

Steve Blackah – what can I say? You never gave up on me, thank you.

All of the above have given selflessly and I will be forever indebted.

I would like to thank all those who have given financially: Rose; Les; Mike and Sarah; Robin and Geraldine, John and Margaret; Rob, Kate and Nicola; Rich and Suzie; Stuart, my house mate; Jonathan and Rachel; Kevin and Tracy; Pete and Pat; and Helen. Thank you also to all those who have given anonymously.

Finally, I would like to thank Ivan and Jean, parents of a good friend no longer with us, Dave Trim.

Ian Rayner

The majority of names in this book have been changed to protect the individuals mentioned.

I felt, however, that the animals would enjoy the publicity, so their names remain completely unchanged.

CONTENTS

CHAPTER ONE
The woman called my mother

The middle-aged woman slouched round the exercise yard, not talking to anyone beyond the odd acknowledgement as she passed. She looked sullen and apathetic, her pale face drawn and her lank brown hair straggling over her shoulders. She seemed out of place among the other much younger, brash inmates, who swaggered round the yard, chattering animatedly and catcalling the prison officers with flirtatious or obscene remarks.

I stared at this woman, forcing myself to accept that she was my mother. I didn't even recognise her. The familiar bitterness, born in my earliest days and nurtured by my grandmother, rose up in me. I felt physically sick.

My own mother, and I didn't even recognise her. It was only because an officer had told me that she was in the Women's Wing, and she was the only one of that age, that I knew it must be her. What irony that she and her son had both ended up inside, except that she didn't know I was here. Should I ask to go and see her? As I brooded over this question, I struggled to get my feelings under control. I had only got this far by not having feelings. It wasn't going to help anything if I suddenly got emotional. But the memories kept coming.

I was four years old and full of excitement because I was outside for once, released from the tedium of our small house. I raced to my beloved tricycle, not bothered about its somewhat tatty and rusty state. It was my trusty steed, taking me off on adventures, transforming itself into all sorts of things – machines, monsters, elephants, racing cars, tanks, dinosaurs. My imagination was exhilarated by the pure delight of speed and risk. But on this occasion, it ended in disaster. Taking a corner too fast, I swerved out of control and pitched right over. With a sickening thud, I hit my head and landed on my back. Once the initial second of shock had passed, the pain and fear kicked in, and I burst into loud screams. I touched my head where it hurt, and looked aghast at the red sticky stuff on my hand. 'Mummy,' I wailed, staggering into the house, shaking with shock.

She was sitting in the front room, surrounded by coffee cups and magazines, the television burbling in the background. Different wails came from the pram in the hall, but neither of us took any notice of them. They were just another normal background noise.

She looked at me without any change of expression. All hope I might have had of a comforting hug and a 'sweetie to make it better' were dashed when she snapped, 'Oh f*** off, you stupid kid. Go and get your Gran to see to you.'

Bewildered, knowing, even in my four-year-old understanding, that this wasn't how things should be, I stumbled off to my Gran's house. My head ached and throbbed, I could hardly see through my tears, but the growing pain deep inside me felt even harder to bear.

Now the memories came thick and fast, relentlessly moving me to the last time I had seen her, standing on the doorstep of a strange house. People shouting and swearing, my brother Joey wailing again. My mother with a hunted look on her face, set and hard. My Dad, desperate, yelling at her to think of the children. A strange man in the house behind her. Confusion and pain.

What had gone wrong? Was I to blame? My agitated mind struggled to make sense of the events that had shaped my life and had brought me to this desperate point.

My parents were a mismatched couple. They had met at a mutual friend's wedding and the relationship had developed from there. It was not particularly serious; neither really wanted commitment at that point. My mother was an office worker, my Dad a labourer, and they were only young. My mother already had a daughter from a previous relationship and just wanted a good time to offset the pressures of single parenthood. It was only the discovery of her pregnancy – me – that jerked the relationship onto a different plane. They married, but my Mum's heart wasn't really in it. The resentment she felt about being tied down and having yet another child to look after transferred itself to me. Almost immediately after birth I was fostered out, as my mother didn't feel she could care for me. After a couple of months, she had a change of heart and decided to have me back.

Mum lapsed into apathy, probably post-natal depression. She neglected her new baby, and gave very little attention to her daughter either. The house was untidy and dirty and echoed to the wailing and whimpering of unhappy children. From the earliest days I was unwanted, resented. Though at first too young to realise this, I nonetheless subconsciously absorbed an attitude of hostility and disconnection. Very early on, I was forced to become self-sufficient emotionally. The barriers to feeling were being erected.

My father made quite good money in a factory in Stockport. He enjoyed his job, and felt glad to be supporting his family so satisfactorily. Soon, however, this was to change. My mother, for once in league with my grandparents, decided that it would be a wonderful idea to go and live on the Isle of Man. The family had been there for a holiday, and understandably had fallen in love with the place.

'We'll all go there,' said Gran. 'It'll be a new start for us.'

'That's as maybe, but will there be work?' said Dad. 'It's not exactly the centre of industry, is it?'

'I've done some investigating,' said my mother, quickly. 'There's a factory which is taking on people right now. Good money, and apparently plenty of housing round there.'

My father, despite some remaining uneasiness, was persuaded to take the plunge, give in his notice and move wife, children, parents, brother and family, and worldly goods to the Isle of Man. It was a lovely place to be, wild, beautiful, friendly and relatively cheap, but there was no job in the factory my mother had mentioned. In fact, she had not done any investigating; talk of work had merely been a ploy to persuade my father to her way of thinking. It was one of the first of many disagreements and tensions that crept into their marriage and finally destroyed it.

It was my father's turn to go through a time of depression. We had arrived in winter, and the bleak weather and dreary landscape reflected his mood and added to it. The flat we had moved into in Peel was in a bad state, with a leaky roof, damp inside and very poor decoration. He had no job and therefore no money. We were reduced to relying on Gran to provide a weekly

Sunday meal. Eventually he found work in the local brick factory on a quarter of his previous wage. The arguments between my parents became part of my life; shouting and fierce silences the norm.

I was an anxious child, despite being normalised to stress and disagreement. At the age of four, two years after we moved to the Isle of Man, I was still bedwetting. I remember the wet, warm sensation when I first woke in the morning, immediately followed by the sinking realisation that I had done it again and Mummy would be cross. Except that often she didn't even notice, and I would return to smelly, damp sheets in the evening, only to repeat the whole process again the next night. I found this strangely hard to bear, and would cry bitterly each night, listening to my parents shouting at each other about it. Why didn't one of them come and change the sheets, give me some comfort and security? I never discovered the answer to this question, and they never came.

I recalled what had begun as a happier day. My Mum had insisted that Dad take Joey and me shopping in the main town of Douglas. Such an unusual treat was to be enjoyed to the full, and we raced around, shrieking with excitement, until she shouted at us to shut up. I asked if Ruth, my older half-sister was coming too. My Dad looked as if he was going to agree, but my Mum said, 'No', very quickly. Ruth began to whine and Dad was about to argue the decision, but Mum got quite fierce. 'She's staying here with me and that's that,' she said.

We sidled towards the door, recognising and fearing the hard edge to her voice. Unexpectedly, she gave us a quick hug goodbye, and then we were off, heading for a rare visit to the town.

Dad seemed to have caught the spirit of the day. 'Come on boys,' he said, 'let's go and see what's in the toyshop.'

We had a wonderful hour in there, gazing in awe at all the amazing treasures, and playing with them whenever possible. Dad was relaxed and smiling. We seemed like an ordinary family. The crowning moment came when he bought me a cowboy suit, complete with toy gun. I was in heaven! I put it on straightaway and played at cowboys for the rest of the afternoon, taking pot-shots at pedestrians as we travelled home on the bus, and rushing up the road to show Mum and Ruth our exciting purchases.

The house was empty. I was puzzled, but far too absorbed in being a cowboy to notice the fear in my Dad's voice as he called for Mum. He looked in every room, then rushed outside, followed by me, shooting the Indians who were holding Mum and Ruth hostage.

'Shut up your noise,' shouted Dad, all trace of his relaxed and smiling manner gone. 'We're going to your Gran's.' We would never again see him quite so happy as he had been that afternoon.

My mother. She had caused such pain. She had walked out of our lives, apparently without a second thought, taking Ruth, but not us. She had taken lots of money too, money my Dad and grandparents said wasn't hers to take.

At my grandparents' house, my Dad was distraught and grim. Joey and I usually loved being there. It felt safe – not this time though. There were raised voices and crying. The air was charged with emotion. Then we were being bundled into the car again, this time with Grandad there as well. We drew up in front of a strange house, where to my surprise, my mother opened the door. I hardly had time to gasp, 'Mummy', when the shouting started. Everyone was yelling at one another, and occasionally we were thrust forward, almost like weapons. I looked from one grown-up to another, not understanding what was going on, just fearing the anger and the uncertainty.

'Don't you use the kids against me,' she yelled. 'Of course I b***** love them. But I've got my own life to think of. You b***** look after them for a change.'

She glared at my father, daring him to do or say something more, and then slammed the door in our faces. I glimpsed a strange man again in the background, moving towards her. Whoever was he?

Dad, Grandad and us two boys stood for a moment on the doorstep, stunned by the ferocity of the incident. Grandad looked as if he was going to throw his considerable weight against the door, but then thought better of it. He and Dad looked at each other and then turned away. My Dad walked slowly with his head down, like a soldier taken prisoner. Grandad picked Joey up and I trailed behind, miserable and frightened, but mostly aware that I was really very hungry. This was the last time I ever saw my mother, until now.

Sitting on my bed in the prison cell, I was churned up with a mixture of emotions. The main one was anger – with her for messing up my life in the past and for getting me into the situation I was in now. I felt as if she was invading my space; I didn't want to have to think about her and deal with all these feelings and memories. For a short while, I allowed myself to imagine what it would be like to meet her, whether we could make up all that was lost, even be friends. But then I snapped the window of possibility shut. She had spoilt enough. I wasn't going to let her rob me of the rest of my life. I told the officers to make sure that we never had contact or they could expect trouble.

So was it my fault that they argued? Was it my fault that she walked out that day with Ruth, leaving my Dad to cope with two forlorn little cowboys? The self-centredness of my child's world meant that I truly believed that somehow I was to blame for what had happened. I felt guilty and confused. Mummy didn't love me enough to stay. It must have been the way I behaved.

She had told me often enough that I was naughty and bad. Here was proof indeed.

We stayed at our grandparents' house. At first it was just meant to be for a few days, but it soon became permanent. Dad had to go out to work, so couldn't look after a four- and a one-year-old. There was no alternative but for Gran and Grandad to take up the reins of the household. It was not what they had envisaged when they moved to their retirement home on the Isle of Man.

My grandmother, protective of her son and grandchildren and left to shoulder the burden of child-rearing for a second time, was bitter and unforgiving. She hated my mother for what she had done, and did not try to hide that hatred from my brother or me. We grew up unable to speak of our mother or ask any questions, aware that she had done something dreadful against all of us, but not really knowing what, or more importantly, why.

I was happy though, because I loved Gran and Grandad, even though they were strict and often impatient and bad-tempered. But I knew they loved me and that made all the difference. I was able to relax and became a lively little boy.

We usually saw Dad at the weekend, and, relieved of most of his responsibilities, he too was more relaxed. He used to play with us for a little while on a Sunday before retreating behind a newspaper. On one occasion, however, he looked quite upset, and didn't want to play.

'Joey's going away for a while,' he said.

'Where? Can I go too?' I asked, fearing as always that I was missing out on something.

'No!' he said sharply. 'It's a place just for babies.'

I was puzzled, not able to imagine such a place. 'Why? He's all right here. He doesn't need a special place.'

Dad's face screwed up a bit. I watched, fascinated. Was he going to cry?

'Your Gran and Grandad are a bit old now for looking after little boys,' he said. 'They can only manage one, so Joey's going to live somewhere else.'

I was only four, but the sense of loss was real, even if I couldn't articulate it. First Mum and Ruth, now Joey, my little ally and admirer, who followed me adoringly and always did what I said. That night, the bedwetting, which had practically ceased, began again.

Months passed, and I grew used to being the only child. We went to visit Joey every so often, but I didn't enjoy the visits. He was in a Children's Home – a large, slightly intimidating building, which smelt of cooking and toilets and had noisy echoes. Joey seemed glad to see us, but he didn't seem like my brother any more. I was always secretly pleased to get back to Gran's house and comparative peace. Grandad was a bit frightening, a gruff, rather bad-tempered man, but I was used to him and knew when to keep out of his way. Gran, for all her complaining and telling off, would do anything for me and I knew it.

One day, while she was cooking the tea, and I was getting under her feet, she said suddenly, 'So, how would you like to go back to live with your Dad again, eh?'

I was astounded. This was home now, and though I loved Dad, and looked forward to seeing him at the weekend, even if only for a short time, I hadn't ever thought about leaving Gran's. 'Has Mummy come back?' I asked cautiously.

Gran's mouth tightened. 'No, nor is she likely to. Your Dad's got someone else to be a Mummy for you.'

This was a new idea, and I didn't think I liked it. Someone else to be Mummy. Someone I didn't even know. 'I don't want to,' I said flatly.

A look of sympathy crossed Gran's face, but she sounded annoyed when she spoke. 'Well, you'll have to put up with it, because your Dad wants you to go back there. He's going to get Joey back as well.'

So that Saturday, my belongings bundled into a suitcase and clutching my favourite toy, I arrived back at Dad's flat. As we drew up outside, I saw two children by the front door.

'Look! Who are they?'

Gran and Grandad exchanged glances. 'You'd think she could have arranged for them to be out when he got here,' said Gran. Grandad grunted. 'Your Dad's new friend, Mary, well, she's already got two children,' said Gran. 'So you're going to be a nice big family, aren't you?'

I thought about this, feeling a tight knot in my stomach. 'Too big!' I announced. 'I'll stay with you, Gran.'

But Gran got out of the car quickly without saying anything, and they lifted me out. The strange children and I stared at one another.

'Come on,' said Grandad, loudly, 'let's go and find your Dad.'

I skirted round the children, who followed me round to the back door. Dad swung me up and gave me a hug, obviously pleased to see me. 'We're all together again, Ian,' he said. 'Your brother's here as well, look.'

Joey was toddling towards me, shouting, 'Dada, Dada.'

'See, he can talk as well,' laughed Dad. 'Now this here is Gemma, and this is Wayne, and **here**', he beamingly swept towards the living-room, 'is Mary.'

I saw a pale face, not really smiling or frowning, with bright blue eyes and streaky brown hair. She was sitting on the sofa, waiting.

'Well, go and give her a kiss hello,' said Dad, a bit impatiently. I walked forward obediently, squirming with embarrassment, but was saved by Mary, who rose to her feet and held out her hand.

'We don't know each other well enough yet for kisses. Shall we shake hands?' she said. Not friendly, but not unfriendly. I put out my hand awkwardly and then ran back to Gran.

'Why don't you go out and play with Gemma and Wayne?' said Dad, determined to be cheerful. 'They're a bit older than you and will look after you.' I looked pleadingly at Gran but she gave me a little shove towards the door, so reluctantly I went outside.

Gemma and Wayne didn't say much, but whispered to each other for a bit. Then Wayne suddenly ran round to the back of the house and reappeared with a football.

'Want to play?' he asked. I nodded nervously. Perhaps it was going to be all right. And it was.

The next few years were comparatively stable. It was odd to have strangers as part of your family, but I got used to it. Joey didn't know any different.

The house itself was crowded and noisy. There was no inside toilet and very little in the way of heating. The bath was in the kitchen and, with a board on top of it, doubled up as a table. Bath time was once a week; usually an occasion of much boisterous play, ending with a very wet kitchen and Mary in a bad mood.

It was good to have Dad around. He was much happier than I had seen him for a long time. He spent quite a bit of time with the four of us and we had fun together. There was the time he spent ages making four boats out of bits of wood, with Penguin wrappers for sails. And another when he played football in the park with us, pretending to be an incompetent goalie and chasing us whenever we scored a goal.

We lived quite near the beach, and I loved being able to go down there to play. One day, I persuaded Mary to let me take a few sandwiches and spend the day there on my own. She agreed, probably glad to have at least one child out of the way. Armed with bucket and spade, I set off.

After a period of wave-dodging and castle-building, I noticed a group of people further up the beach, standing near a banner. Curious, I ran along the beach towards the crowd. There was a man standing on a small portable stage, with a large easel next to him. He was talking and drawing at the same time. Fascinated, I drew closer.

'... so although they were having a great time in the garden,' the man was saying, drawing a tree, flowers, birds and butterflies very rapidly, 'they were curious to know more.' He drew a large, smiling snake. 'So, when this charming creature started chatting to Eve, telling her that there was a tree that could give her great wisdom and knowledge, she was interested. But she remembered that God had told them not to eat from that particular tree. "Oh really?" purred the snake. "Did God **really** say that? He just doesn't want you to be equal with him. Go on, take a bite."'

The man paused dramatically, and we all waited, enthralled. Would Eve take a bite; what would happen? We listened as the man, a gifted storyteller, told and illustrated the rest of the story – the persuading of Adam to eat as well, the sudden realisation of the enormity of what they had done, the loss of innocence and intimate relationship with God, who could no longer allow them to remain in the garden. To my childish ears, it was a very sad story, with an unsatisfactory ending. They didn't live happily ever after.

The man explained that eventually, after many many thousands of years, God did make a happy ending, but I didn't really understand. The cold and my short attention span took over, and I scampered back through the waves to where I'd left my bag and food. The story stayed with me though. The episode with the storyteller added to a golden day.

Gradually, it dawned on me that family life was not as happy or settled as I'd unthinkingly assumed. Slowly, the number of arguments between Mary and Dad increased. She always seemed to be cross or complaining about something. However hard I tried to please her, I never seemed to succeed. The added burden of looking after a toddler again was not to her liking.

'I've been through all this twice, and I don't want to go through it again,' was her often repeated phrase, as she tried in vain to persuade Joey to use the potty, mopped up sick and battled to contain his tantrums. 'You do it; they're **your** children,' was something else we heard frequently.

Dad did what he could, but he was working long hours and wasn't around to care for us. Mary, it seemed, didn't want to.

Late one night, there was loud shouting from downstairs. Mary was going on at length, her voice rising and falling in a litany of complaints. Whenever my Dad (also shouting) interrupted, she would just continue more loudly, usually with the words, 'And that's **another** thing ...' Finally, having worked herself up into a state, she blurted out what had clearly always been at the root of the whole issue. 'Well, it's them or me. You choose. Either they go, or I do.'

There was an appalled silence.

'But Mary, they're my kids. I want them with me.'

'You can still see them. I just don't want them here any more. I mean it John. I'm at the end of my tether. If they stay, I go. I've had enough.'

That weekend, Joey went back to the Children's Home, and I went back to my grandparents' house.

CHAPTER TWO
Changing families

From my special den, I watched the smart lady come out of the house and walk briskly down the path, her high heels clicking on the concrete. She opened up her gleaming car, put her handbag in and drove off with a roar of exhaust, watched by a gang of gawping kids.

'Ian, come here, I've got something to say,' Gran called from the house. I wriggled out of my den, hoping the kids wouldn't spot where it was, and went inside. Gran looked strange.

'Have you been crying, Gran?' I'd only seen her cry once before, when my mother left. What disaster had happened now?

But she brushed her eyes impatiently and said, 'Don't be silly. Now, a lady's just been round with some exciting news.' I wrinkled my brow. She didn't sound excited. Sad more like. 'Your little brother, Joey, isn't going to live in the Children's Home any more. He's being adopted.' My frown deepened.

'What's adopted?'

'It means that a family who want a little boy have chosen him to be their child. That lady is going to be his new Mummy.'

'But he's ours! Mine and Dad's and yours! Someone else can't have him.'

Gran swallowed. She seemed to be having trouble speaking. 'Your Dad can't look after him, and neither can we, so your Dad thought it would be better for him to have another family than to stay in the Children's Home.'

I could see the sense in that. I still hated visiting the Home. 'Will we still be able to go and see him?'

She looked at me and again I thought she was going to burst into tears. But she smiled grimly and said, 'Better than that. The people adopting Joey think it would be lovely if you and Joey could be together again and they could have a ready-made family. So you're going to go and live there too.'

I felt my eight-year-old world, so carefully put back together, come crashing down around me. 'No, Gran. I don't want to. I want to stay here with you and Grandad. I like it here. And Joey could come and visit us sometimes.'

She sighed. 'I'm sorry, love. They think it's for the best if you go.'

I bit my lower lip, to stop myself crying. 'Who thinks that? Who's "they"?'

'The man who wants to adopt you, Geoff, went round and chatted to your Dad in the pub. They agreed that it would be good for you and Joey to live as brothers again. Geoff and his wife want more than an only child, so this suits everyone. Geoff and your Dad shook hands on it.'

I was silent for a while, feeling betrayed, as if I was a deal to shake hands on. My own Dad was giving me away in the pub. I felt a hard lump inside me. 'Do **you** think it's for the best?' I said at last.

'It's not up to me, Ian,' she said wearily, suddenly looking like an old lady.

The next few days were like a bad dream. We packed up my few belongings and Gran wrote a list of my likes and dislikes. I said goodbye to my friends on the street and at school. I was moving to a different town and so to a different school. Up until then, school hadn't featured very much in my life; a place one was forced to attend and which was frequently boring, sometimes frightening. All of a sudden it became very attractive and secure. The thought of starting again in a new place where I knew no one, not even the people I was living with, was terrifying.

When the time came, I was yet again bundled into the car and taken to a new home. Inside, I was feeling sick and shaky, but on the outside, I sat silent, determined not to show anyone how much I cared. It was some distance over the hills to the next town, and with every passing mile, I felt more and more isolated. Finally we arrived at a huge place set on a hill, overlooking the town of Douglas.

'Geoff and Maureen run a hotel,' said Gran, answering my unspoken question. 'You'll have plenty of space and nice toys. You'll like it, I bet.' I wasn't so sure, but I kept silent, climbing out of the car and standing uncertainly on the drive.

'Ian! Ian!' A small boy ran towards me, beaming with delight. It was Joey. I hadn't seen him for quite a while and he had grown tremendously. 'I go to school now!' he said proudly. I wanted to put my arms round him, but felt embarrassed in front of strangers.

A tall man with a beard came towards me, smiling. The smart lady I had seen at our house followed him. She was quite small (no high heels this time), with wavy brown hair and lots of lipstick. 'Hello, Ian. I'm Geoff, and this is Maureen. Welcome to your new home.'

Maureen gave me a hug, which I didn't enjoy. We all went into the hotel's grand hall. Another lady was sitting behind a desk, but Geoff and Maureen walked straight past her and into a large living-room. I gazed around in awe. I couldn't believe that someone's house could have such big rooms. Joey was racing round and round in a frenzy of excitement. Gran frowned warningly at him, but Geoff and Maureen watched him indulgently, thrilled to see him so happy there.

I clung to Gran as she went, wanting more than anything to go back with her, but she couldn't take me. Her eyes were full of tears as she turned away after a last hug.

'I'll see you soon, Gran!' I shouted desperately after her, fighting back my own tears. She waved, but didn't reply. Dejectedly, I watched the car drive away, then turned towards the huge, comfortless building that I had to learn to call home.

The next few months were bleak. At one level, I quickly settled in and made the most of the space and luxury I had never known before. I had never had so many toys and clothes, and the food was incredible, both in variety and content. I ate like a little pig for the first week or so, until I realised that it wasn't going to go away. Geoff and Maureen (or 'dad' and 'mum' as they preferred to be called) were constantly giving me new things, watching intensely until I had expressed delight and thanks.

But somehow, even at that young age, I knew they were trying to buy my love and acceptance. I took their things, but I didn't feel any love for them or from them. I was lonely and homesick for Gran. Geoff and Maureen were kind but not demonstrative towards me. They treated me as they might a friend's child, friendly but a bit detached, and reserved their warmth and care for Joey, who lapped up their affection and returned it with interest.

Joey, indeed, seemed very happy. The hotel must have seemed like heaven after the Children's Home. He wasn't old enough to remember our mother, and even memories of Dad, Gran and Grandad were hazy, because he had not lived with them for sufficient time. Recently, they had just become some of the many adults visiting the Children's Home. Now, he had two people almost exclusively to himself, who gave him lots of love, attention, toys and books. And he only had to share a bedroom with one other person – me. Sometimes, I thought I was only there as another way of meeting Joey's needs. It was good for him to have a brother to play with and do things with, so here I was. I got on all right with him, but he was only five, and I missed my old friends.

I didn't like my new school, or the children in it. They stared and giggled at me in the playground and left me out of their activities. The 'don't care' attitude that had been growing in me since I left Gran's became more developed at school. I would show them that I wasn't bothered if they laughed at me or picked on me.

I gradually found a few boys with whom I could rub along, and we became the naughty gang. I discovered that I really didn't care much about being told off or upsetting people. The hard lump I had first felt when I heard that my Dad had given me away in the pub had become solid, blocking the feelings of sadness, loneliness and fear and only allowing out feelings of anger and dislike.

My new parents didn't know how to deal with me. They sensed my indifference to them and felt hurt that their efforts to woo me didn't succeed in creating love. Their experience of children was limited and they didn't know how to deal with this surly eight-year-old whose behaviour was becoming increasingly unacceptable.

One day, Joey and I were taken to the local court house and made to sit around while Geoff and Maureen and some other people talked a lot and signed papers. Afterwards we went to a café for a drink. I was quite happy, because this seemed a far better thing to be doing than Maths. Everyone else was in school, and we were in town having a drink!

'There, you're both properly adopted now,' said Maureen. 'You're our little boys forever.'

Joey smiled, enjoying the atmosphere of happiness, but I remained straight-faced. Maureen looked at me anxiously, but pressed on. 'So you've got a new name and a new family.'

'Aren't I called Ian any more then?' I asked, puzzled.

Geoff laughed. 'Course you are, silly,' he said, ruffling my hair. 'It's your last name, the family name, which changes.'

I shifted away from him. 'I don't want to be called Robertson. I like my own name. Besides, there's already someone called that at school and he's horrible.'

Geoff and Maureen exchanged glances and Geoff said firmly, 'Well, don't worry about it now, you'll get used to it. Everyone who's adopted takes on the name of their new family.'

I stood up, feeling sick again. 'C'mon, let's go. I want to get back to school.'

I hated my new name with intensity. I hated the way the children whispered and looked when the register was taken. I hated Ben Robertson's smirk when our books got mixed up. I felt robbed of my original surname, as if an important part of who I was had been taken away, as well as the last link with my Gran, my Dad and my past.

I also hated the fact that Geoff expected me to take on his likes and dislikes along with his name. I even had to support his favourite football team. Everton! As if I ever would! He bought me all the kit, and made sure I wore it when I watched matches with him or went out to play footie with my mates. I felt that they were trying to change me completely, into someone who wasn't me at all.

The worst thing of all was that I was not allowed to have contact with my Gran and Grandad any more. I wanted to see Gran so badly, but they wouldn't let me. Maureen said that it would unsettle me and make it more difficult for me to feel at home with them. I wasn't even allowed to send or receive presents from them at Christmas or on birthdays. The first few times this happened, I made a real fuss about it, feeling hurt inside at the loss of my grandparents. But Geoff and Maureen could not be persuaded to change their minds, so I didn't let them see how much it bothered me. Without even realising, I pushed away the feelings of loss and hurt and concentrated on expressing indifference and defiance. The emotional barriers were growing higher and higher.

My behaviour got worse and Geoff and Maureen reacted with increasingly harsh punishments. They were trying to break through the barrier of unresponsiveness I had built round myself but found it impossible. I had pretended for so long that I didn't care that it was beginning to come true. But I resented the beltings and the groundings, refusing to acknowledge that my behaviour had contributed to the situation.

One Christmas Day, after I had been deliberately disobedient, I was made to stand in the corner until I apologised. I was determined not to do so, and stood there for four hours, until finally being sent to bed.

On another occasion, as I was waiting, petrified, for Geoff to come and punish me for something I had done wrong – something inside me snapped. I couldn't stand it any longer. I ran to the back of the house, crawled out of the window and up the bank, which climbed steeply away from the hotel. Terrified that I would hear shouts behind me at any moment, I raced upwards, my heart pounding and my breath coming in short, uneven bursts. Finally, I was well out of sight and onto the railway line. I knew this line went to Peel, my grandparents' town, so I reasoned that if I just followed it along, I would get there eventually. But I hadn't reckoned on the fork in the line.

I took what I thought was the correct line and trudged on, imagining the look of delight on Gran's face when I turned up. After a few miles, though, I realised that I was lost. Above me, dark trees towered, their branches creaking scarily in the wind. I shivered, and for the first time wondered if I was going to make it to Gran's. No sooner was the thought in my head than I started to panic. I looked around wildly, wondering how I could get out of there. It was too far to go back, and besides, I was still sure I could get to Gran's if only I could be certain of the direction.

Suddenly I spotted a small coal yard, taken over, I suppose, from the days of steam and now run as a small business. I clambered up the embankment to it, and realised that the only way out onto the road was from the top of a pile of coal. This normally would have been a fun activity, but in the failing light, with threatening trees all around, I felt scared and alone. My foot slipped several times, sending cascades of coal rattling to the bottom. Finally, I reached the top, stepped onto the wall and dropped down onto the verge on the other side. Covered in coal dust and shaking with the exertion and fear I started up the road, in what I hoped was the right direction.

I had been walking for about half an hour, without recognising any landmarks, when a car went past slowly, then stopped just a bit further up the road. I froze. All the warnings about strangers and cars flooded back to me. The door opened, and a woman got out.

'Ian? Is that you?' she called. 'Whatever are you doing here?'

It was a friend of Geoff and Maureen's. She took one look at the state of me and asked no more questions, instead popping me into the car and driving me back to the hotel. All the way back, I was panicking about what would happen to me when I arrived.

Fortunately, they were so relieved to see me safe that I didn't receive the punishment I expected. For quite some time, however, there was a wary truce between us. As time passed, the hardness that was protecting me from loneliness and hurt gradually grew.

The continued non-contact with my Gran was the most difficult thing to bear, but I even built a barrier there. My behaviour started to reflect this inner hardness and I began to do some seriously naughty things.

It was at this time that I began to experiment with smoking, taking cigarettes from the hotel and creeping round the back to try them. I also stole bottles of pop and chocolate whenever I could. I enjoyed my adopted lifestyle of possessions, clothes and nice holidays, but I could not accept Geoff and Maureen as parents. Though I never actually said as much, they knew that at a fundamental level, the adoption had failed.

I continued to loathe school, and my teachers seemed to reciprocate the feeling. My increasingly challenging behaviour – answering back, getting into fights, refusing to work, disrupting classes – meant that I was not an easy child to relate to. Some teachers tried, but I wouldn't respond. Other teachers made their dislike of me quite obvious. One was even mean enough to tell me, in front of the whole class, that I would never amount to anything. Outwardly, I pretended not to care, merely muttering loudly, 'Like you then, Miss.' Inwardly, though, I was burning with humiliation and resentment. Her words were to remain with me for many years.

When I was ten, I once again decided that I'd had enough. Though I was superficially settled, the passing of time had not reconciled me to these people who didn't really love me, and who punished me without leniency. I tolerated them, and enjoyed the practical care they gave, but emotionally, I could not accept them, or the home they had provided. I made plans to escape.

This time, I did not intend to get lost and frightened. I arranged a date with a friend, Simon, and talked him into coming with me. It was a great adventure. We only had one bike, so at about seven o'clock on the morning of 'the Escape', I broke into the shed of a friend who lived on the road leading out of town, and stole his bike. Thus, equipped with a stolen racer, and my chopper (which was stuck in third gear), we set off over the hills to the other side of the island.

It was about a 12-mile journey, and the hills were quite steep in places. Sometimes, it felt as if we were climbing Mount Everest! But I was determined to do it, and kept spurring Simon on when he was inclined to give up and go home. He, after all, didn't have my motivation – he had a home to go to at the end of the day.

Finally, after about four hours, we breasted the last hill and saw the sea ahead, and Peel, with its harbour and castle, sprawling along the coastline. We'd done it! With whoops of delight, we freewheeled down and then, with me in the lead, pedalled towards my Gran and Grandad's house. It was only as we approached that a flicker of fear flashed through my elation. What if they sent me straight back? Or called the police? What if they didn't want me? But I refused to entertain such thoughts, and pressed on, confident that my Gran would be overwhelmed with delight when she saw me.

We abandoned our bikes and rushed round to the back door. I burst in, suddenly feeling shaky and emotional, and yelled, 'Gran! Where are you? I'm back!'

I heard the sound of someone coming downstairs, the door opened and there she was, her face full of astonishment. 'Ian!' she gasped. 'What ... how ... . Oh, I can't believe it!' We ran to each other and she enclosed me in a huge hug.

'Gran! I can't bear it! I want to live with you. Please let me. Don't make me go back.'

Without realising it, I was crying, sobbing into her comforting bulk. All the tensions and exertions of the day, all the unhappiness of the past years came flowing out. She made soothing noises, just like when I was four years old with a cut head. As my sobs subsided, I realised that Simon was standing there, looking very embarrassed.

The rest of the day passed in bustle and confusion. I could hear phone calls being made and received. Simon's parents came to pick him up, looking very annoyed. Grandad came home, stared at me in amazement, and after a word or two, stomped off to discuss the situation with Gran. Geoff and Maureen arrived, looking distraught. They spoke to me for a bit, then disappeared into the front room, where a loud discussion followed. I could hear people arguing, and at one point someone was crying. I heard Geoff shout, 'Well, God knows we've tried. We'll have him back, but there's no point if he hates it so much.'

Grandad sounded angry as he replied, and I heard Gran trying to calm him down a bit. The talking went on and on and then at last, the door opened and Geoff and Maureen came out. Maureen's eyes were red and puffy and Geoff's face was pale and set. They came up to where I was sitting and looked down at me.

'OK, Ian. You win,' said Geoff, gruffly. 'If you really want to stay here you can. We've done our best but obviously it wasn't enough.'

I wanted to say that it wasn't really their fault, but nothing came out. Maureen looked as if she was going to cry again.

'Well, then,' said Geoff again, after a short silence. 'We'd better get back to Joey. He'll miss you, Ian.'

I swallowed. This was the hardest bit.

'Best not come and visit him yet though. It'll upset him too much. Take care, then.'

He turned to go. Maureen gave a little cry, brushed a kiss on the top of my head and they were gone.

At last, I was back where I wanted to be. But as the days stretched to weeks and months, I realised that achieving my goal was not turning out to be as wonderful as I thought. Though I was secure in my Gran's love, I found her a lot more impatient and short-tempered than I remembered. As for my grandfather, he made it fairly obvious from the beginning that he didn't want me living there. He kept making comments about me throwing away a good chance in life, and how he was too old to start again bringing up kids. Gran kept telling him to stop, and she did her very best to make me feel at home, but that niggling, insecure feeling of being unwelcome persisted. I began to spend a great deal of time out of the house, hanging around on the streets with a gang of friends from the 'old days'.

Another symptom of my insecurity was that I was still bedwetting. This was a source of constant humiliation to me, especially when I started at

Secondary School. Often, I would wake up in the morning with only ten minutes spare to catch the bus. There was no time to get a bath and so I would put my uniform on over the stale urine, and arrive, smelly and defensive. Memories of all those childhood nights, lying on wet, smelly sheets burnt into me as I sauntered in, trying not to care. I hated it so much, but couldn't seem to stop it. My grandfather used to get very angry when he saw my Gran putting yet more bedding through the wash. It never occurred to them to take me to the doctor's about it. Nor did I seem capable of getting up a bit earlier in order to wash myself thoroughly before school. Such a shameful problem just made me more angry and hard inside and ready to 'have a go' at anyone who seemed to be picking on me.

The streets of Peel didn't offer much amusement to restless youngsters. We decided to make our own entertainment. This took the form of anything that gave us a thrill and got the adrenalin rushing. At first, there were the usual mischievous activities such as knock and run, egging and the like, but then we became bored and started doing more and more daring things. From the outset, I emerged as the natural ringleader on these adventures; a role which I relished – until we got into trouble.

One day, as we were loitering on the street, we spotted a parked lorry. Having used it as target practice for clods of earth, we decided that it would be fun to see if we could smash the windows. My two mates restricted themselves to the side windows, but I decided that the windscreen presented a far better challenge. As the glass shattered into a thousand pieces, we gasped with suppressed laughter and excitement and raced away from the scene of the crime. Later that day, the police questioned one of my friends. How could they have known? No one was about at the time. My friend, not as streetwise as me, confessed almost immediately and also named me as the instigator. I was taken to court and fined £52, payable in instalments.

My grandparents were furious. I kept out of Grandad's way as much as possible, fearing a hiding, but still had to endure Gran's severe telling off. Every week, for the next six months, she dragged me up to the Police Station to pay the fine, scolding and nagging me the whole way. At first, I hated the whole procedure, but after a few weeks, I couldn't care less, and even enjoyed it if I met some of my mates on the way.

Sometimes, in the early days of being back there, I wished that Gran would talk to me about the way I was behaving and the amount of time I was out on the streets. Perhaps I even wanted to be treated more strictly **before** I did anything wrong, rather than afterwards. Subconsciously, I wanted her to make me stay in the house with her. But she didn't. Her discipline was confined to telling me off after the event; a constant sniping of criticisms and reproaches, aimed at making me feel guilty. Unfortunately, as time went by, they came to have the opposite effect. I spent more and more time with my mates, devising increasingly serious diversions in an effort to create some excitement and fulfilment in our lives.

We discovered alcohol in a big way during this period. One evening we decided quite deliberately that we wanted to find out what it would be like to get drunk. We crept round to the back of the local pub and managed to break into the cellar. We all grabbed as much as we could, hardly daring to breathe as we did so. Creeping back up the stairs, terrified that someone would drop a bottle, we loaded our contraband onto a handy wheelbarrow and fled to our den – an abandoned Jag left on some waste ground. We already felt drunk with excitement and bravado, worthy descendants of the great local smuggling tradition. We gazed for a moment at our haul of beer and spirits and then got stuck in.

This was the first of many sessions when my friends and I got totally intoxicated. Stealing drink and then getting drunk became routine. After a while, it was impossible to recapture that initial thrill and we began to get bored and look for some other way to create it. I was developing a pattern which was to control my life for a long time to come; the need for excitement, quickly satiated, leading to searches for new, ever more intense experiences.

We tried glue sniffing, buying up stocks of Evostick, until I could sniff and black out, then wake up somewhere else entirely. Once, after sniffing glue, I found myself walking down the middle of a busy shopping street, with absolutely no recollection of how I got there. It was a scary feeling, but strangely quite pleasurable too. The fuzziness in my head was preferable to the rage and fear I constantly battled against.

At school, I often stole bottles of Tipp-Ex from the teachers' desks in order to sniff them at the end of the day. Some of this was bravado, to gain the admiration of my mates, but some of it was also a pressing need to fill my life with experiences that helped me ignore the hard cancer of anger, fear and rejection inside me.

It was thus a small step from smoking, getting drunk and sniffing glue, to taking drugs. I took the step willingly, casually even, not realising or caring what a painful, dangerous path stretched ahead. And no one tried to stop me.

.

CHAPTER THREE
Drunkenness, drugs and dropping out

The stolen van bumped crazily along the dark track. At age 13, none of us were expert drivers, but we knew enough to keep it going. We made a regular visit to this particular van, and knew it well, always returning it to its parking space after use. This evening, though, had got off to a bad start. The owner of the van, obviously suspecting something, had wired up the steering wheel, so that when Jim (who had been chosen as driver because he was the tallest) first started it, he got an almighty electric shock. It had taken quite a lot of urgent talking to persuade him to continue, and when we finally got going, we careered along with the disconnected wire still sparking as it moved around.

'Watch out! We're getting near!' shouted Gavin above the engine noise. Jim put his foot on the brake and we jolted to a halt.

'Right, we'll leave it here like we did last time,' I said, taking the lead as usual. 'No talking once we're out of the van.'

We eased the doors open and dropped down to the track, checking that no one was around. We scurried along the verge towards the black building silhouetted against the skyline. Panting slightly, I put my shoulder against the thick door and eased the latch. Great! It was open. No need to break in through a window this time. Signing to Jim to keep watch outside, I crept into the building, followed by Gavin. There was an eerie glow inside, coming from the candles on the altar. We hurried down the aisle towards a small room at the side.

'Quick, get the keys out,' whispered Gavin urgently.

I nodded impatiently, hurried to where we had discovered the keys were hidden and fitted them into the safe's lock. The door swung open and we began grabbing the money that was inside. Just at that moment, a bang echoed through the building. We froze, the money in our hands. Jim?

Before we had time to react, there was another bang as the vestry door burst open and Jim was indeed standing there. Behind him, holding him very tightly by the scruff of his neck, was a big policeman. Gavin and I panicked and turned to run, but there was nowhere to go. Another policeman appeared in the main part of the church, and by the door was another. They had been 'staking out' the church for three days, waiting for us. Silently, we climbed into the waiting police van, dreading to think what our families would say when they found out.

We were not let off lightly. We had already committed several minor misdemeanours and were known to the police. Also, it was obvious that we had stolen several times from that particular church. My Gran cried, my Grandad glowered as I was led off to begin six weeks' detention. I made a face at the judge as I went out, but inside I was terrified.

It was an unpleasant experience. I had to get used to a rigorous regime; getting up and going to bed early, unappetising meals at set times, hard school work, constant chores around the centre, strict, unfriendly officers. There was nothing in the way of comfort or leisure time and certainly no privacy. It was no more than I deserved, but I didn't see it that way.

Especially traumatic were the encounters with a prison officer who had more than a professional interest in young boys. He never actually touched me but the consciousness of his eyes on me, the experience of seeing him watch as I took a bath or shower created great fear in me. I was only just entering puberty, and this early encounter with perverted sexuality was very damaging. Eventually, some other boys and I spoke to the chaplain about the problem. He said he didn't believe us, but he must have taken some action, because after that, the officer no longer supervised any bath or bed routines.

Perhaps because of this and other stresses, I found that the habit I had previously developed of frequently needing a 'high' of some sort, was even more pressing in the detention centre. I had to become quite creative to satisfy the need. One of the chores was mowing the lawns, which gave me access to petrol. I managed quite a few sniffs of this, to the detriment of the lawns. I also stole teabags from the kitchen and tried to make them into cigarettes back in my room. Pages torn from the Gideon Bible proved to be the most suitable material, but unfortunately, they didn't stick well and, as always, there was the problem of burnt lips to contend with.

Diversions like this, while not very helpful, at least kept me busy, and the six weeks passed reasonably quickly. I was scared to go back to school, embarrassed because I knew that everyone would stare and talk about me. I was even more scared to go back home, knowing how furious my grandparents were with me. But as always, when there was a real crisis, my Gran supported me. She shielded me from Grandad's ranting and gave me the confidence to go back to school. Although Gran often nagged me and reproached me for my behaviour, I knew that she loved me and would defend me against the world – even when I didn't deserve it. She was my only security.

But this wasn't enough to keep me from the path I had started on. Within a very short time after my return from the detention centre, I had reverted to my old pattern of life. I spent most of my spare time out with my mates, hanging around the streets, getting drunk on stolen booze, sniffing solvents and using pot when we could get hold of it. Petty crime became our normal means of making money and the main aim of our existence was to get as much excitement as possible.

Nothing at school helped to change my ways. Though I was in middle sets, and could have succeeded academically, I was not interested. School could not hold the stimulation that my peer group activities did. Also, school was a source of embarrassment. I was still bedwetting and petrified that someone would find out. Often, I was picked on for being smelly, and people didn't want to sit next to me. I took to spraying deodorant on myself to disguise the smell, and aggressively turned on anyone who made comments.

At the same time, my relationship with my grandfather was deteriorating. He had never been an easy person to get on with, and had long resented having to look after a child again when he should have been enjoying the fruits of old age. Now, though, he became constantly critical, finding fault with everything I did, and calling me horrible names. Never one to accept opposition meekly, I retaliated, not respecting his age or authority. We had some dreadful rows, with Gran trying to intervene, her face drawn with distress and anxiety. Sometimes, perhaps in an effort to put things right, he would suggest a game of table tennis, but these would usually degenerate into quite violent affairs. He would blast the ball across the table, as if he was putting all his anger and dislike into the stroke. I would respond in kind and the ball would travel back and forth like a bullet. Eventually, I was able to beat him and the games became less frequent.

As the years passed, my behaviour got worse at school and in the town, which made my grandfather even more angry and critical. The rows got worse and I spent more and more time away from the house. I stayed out as late as possible at night to avoid him. One night, drunk and depressed, I slept the night in a friend's outside toilet rather than go home. And so the vicious circle was complete; my behaviour, which caused trouble at home, worsened as a result of being on the streets so much, but I stayed out on the streets because of the atmosphere at home. My friends and I egged one another on, and part of my motivation was a desire to get even with Grandad.

On the cliffs just next to our fishing town was an old castle. Although it was locked up at night, it naturally acted as a magnet to the local youth. We liked fishing from the breakwaters with old rods, and would often use the excuse of night-time fishing to stay out very late. We gathered together as much drink as we could find and then broke into the castle to get totally drunk. During one of these sessions, we started telling one another ghost stories. At first, they were just a joke, and in our drunken state, we laughed uproariously and interjected with flippant or obscene remarks. After a while though, as we quietened a bit, and became aware of the dark, looming walls and shifting shadows of history all around us, we began to get a bit edgy and scared. The stories were no longer funny, but intense and frightening.

Suddenly, from deeper within the castle, there was a bang. With shouts of shock and fear, we all leapt to our feet and staggered to the place where we had climbed up over the wall. I was the last to get there and, determined not to be left there on my own, didn't wait to climb down the wall where the footholds were. Instead, I stood on the top and leapt off – dropping 20 feet. I landed with a bump, hurting my back and hitting my head hard against something. I lost consciousness momentarily and came round to hear my mates laughing and jeering and urging me to get up before we got caught. I stood up, and saw that Gavin, my partner in crime, was also being helped up. I had landed on him and knocked him out as well. As we started walking away, we both lurched forward and fell over again, to renewed laughter from our unsympathetic, still drunk friends. While we had been unconscious, they had pulled down our trousers so that whenever we tried to walk, we tripped up!

Apparently none the worse from this incident, or maybe numbed from its effects by the drink, we decided that the night was yet young. We went down to the sea front, stole some rowing boats to get us across the harbour and took it in turns to row crazily towards the fishing area, drinking and tossing the empties overboard. When we got to the other side, we kicked a few fish around and then one of my friends picked up a mackerel and slapped me round the face with it. I immediately retaliated with my own fish, and before long, a full-scale (no pun intended!) fish fight was in progress, accompanied by howls of laughter and mock battle cries. It ended hurriedly when we spotted some irate fishermen heading our way. I don't remember getting home that night, but when I woke up the next morning, I was still dressed, had a fish down my sweater and was black and blue with bruises from my 20-foot fall.

Such escapades became the norm for us. If we didn't get drunk or 'high' and do crazy things, then we didn't think we had succeeded in having a good night out. Life was flat and boring if we didn't inject it with some thrills and spills. The trouble was that as time went by we needed more and more to push out the limits of our daring to achieve the same sensation of thrill and excitement. The lows after the highs became deeper and required more combating. We needed more and more money to fund our endless quest for the next adrenalin rush.

I left school as soon as I could, and got a job as assistant green keeper with the local golf course. It was good, in that I liked to be outdoors and, to some extent, be my own boss. Sometimes, however, I had a bit too much freedom. I found a good supply of magic mushrooms all around the course, which I used to pick in the morning, and make into a flask of 'tea' at lunchtime. One afternoon, having been given the task of mowing nine greens, I decided to have a cup of my 'special tea' before I started. The mowing commenced, but after a very short while, I felt as if I was floating on a huge green sea. The undulations on the course appeared like waves, washing over me, and it was becoming a real battle to get from one end of the green to the other. After two less than satisfactory attempts, I looked back across the green to admire my workmanship. To my shock I saw mower tracks weaving in large curves across the green. I resigned myself to the inescapable fact that this task was too big for me, as the huge green sea was far too rough! Luckily, one of my mates agreed to finish the job off for me. I spent the rest of the afternoon hiding in the bracken – a favourite place of mine on sunny days for sunbathing and smoking pot.

I was out nearly every night drinking, which didn't please my grandparents. They decided to involve my Dad when one night I came home from a particularly heavy drinking session with my workmates. My mates dropped me, literally, on the doorstep, in an unconscious state. Gran heard the commotion and came to the door. Somehow, she managed to drag me up the stairs and onto my bed, where I was promptly sick. When I eventually came to – the next day – I saw that my face was red raw, as if I had been hit hard. Upon going downstairs, my grandparents, still angry, started scolding me and told me that they had called my Dad to the house the previous night to help them deal with me. He had hit me round the face, perhaps in an effort to wake me. I was furious that he should treat me in this way, feeling that he had no right to have this kind of input into my life. I was so angry that I didn't even want to speak to him, so I wrote him a letter, telling him how I felt. He didn't reply.

One evening, when I was about 16, I came back late, rather the worse for wear from drink and pot, and found Grandad still up. There was an empty beer glass and several cans on the table. Normally, I just staggered upstairs and collapsed on the bed. This time, though, Grandad was not going to let me do that. He started shouting at me – ugly, unrepeatable words of accusation and anger. I shouted back, telling him to stay out of my life, enraged that he didn't seem to care or understand.

He strode towards me, face dark with emotion. 'How dare you talk to me like that!' he roared. 'You no hope little b******. You've ruined our lives and you're not wanted. Why don't you f*** off out of here?'

He pushed me so hard that I stumbled against the stairs. Something snapped inside me and with a yell, I lunged towards him. I was vaguely aware that Gran had come down and was begging me to stop. But I couldn't. I grabbed Grandad and pinned him against the wall, shouting all my frustration and hurt at him. I wanted to smack him in the face, but something stopped me. I just kept shouting. Finally, Gran's pleading reached into my consciousness and I let go abruptly, stormed upstairs and gave vent to my feelings by kicking the plasterboard wall of my room so hard that my foot went through several times.

After such a violent encounter, it was hard to resume normal life again. Forgiveness didn't come easily in our family, and neither Grandad nor I would apologise. The incident was not referred to and we relapsed into a silent, uneasy truce. But I'd had enough. Very soon afterwards, I arranged to move out of Gran's house to live in a house in the town. She was worried for me, but acknowledged that the situation at home was impossible. She would have been even more worried if she had known that the household I was moving into comprised two much older men who were habitual drug-users. I often referred to them as 'leftovers from the Sixties'. I got to know them through a mate who smoked a lot of pot and who had heard that I was having trouble at home. It seemed to be a great solution to my problem at the time, but in moving away from Gran, I lost my last moral restraint. Now there was nothing to hold me back from the excesses caused by drink and drugs.

Drug using, drunkenness, heavy smoking, theft, violence – they became the established pattern of my life. The seeds of such a lifestyle had been planted in preceding years, but now they took root. Values that most people called normal were no longer part of my existence. The only norm was getting high, and all the implications that went with it. Living was self-centred, with no moral standards. Of course, I still did right by my mates, but I didn't really trust anyone. Nor did I really care about anyone either.

Throughout this time, I didn't see much of Gran, nor did I go to work very often. This was partly because during the year I was with these two guys, I had two more stretches in the detention centre. I still hated it in there, but it didn't act as a deterrent. I just saw it as a necessary evil, to be endured.

I continued in the nomadic existence I had unwillingly lived since early childhood. After a year I moved on, to a place in Douglas, the main town on the island. A floating population of up to a dozen people of roughly my own age occupied this house; misfits, drop-outs, runaways, truants. Nearly everyone was a drug-user, or had some sort of addiction. There was a constant supply of stolen alcohol, cigarettes and dope and every night seemed to be a party. We were never sure just how many people were resident in the house, because there were always people crashing out in it. Yet there were no close relationships. In all the time I lived there, I never really got to know any of my house mates beyond the superficial. This didn't bother me at all; in fact, I never even thought about it. Life was not about people, and that's how I liked it.

We needed more cash than we had income for the wild lives we were living, which meant resorting to crime. I continued committing theft and burglaries, and added to my repertoire attempts at credit card fraud. There was no thought for the victims of my crime. I had no conscience about what I was doing and never really saw it as harming people. We had our own loose code of conduct which meant that you didn't steal from your own, interweaved with vague ideas based on the Robin Hood principle of robbing the rich to help the poor. We, of course, were the poor.

I had a clear memory of my mother saying to me when I was about four, 'It's all right to steal as long as you don't steal everything. Always leave something behind.' For a long time, I kept to that rule, and always left something behind, almost as a superstition. Then I got to the point where I just stole everything I could get my hands on, shrugging off the only 'value' I remember my mother passing on to me.

It was inevitable that I would eventually get caught, and I did. I was convicted of credit card fraud and sentenced to three months imprisonment, this time in a 'real' prison rather than a detention centre. It was my rite of passage to adulthood. Perversely, I even felt proud of myself, though still found the experience of being 'inside' truly traumatic.

After two months of the sentence, one of the probation officers asked to have a chat with me. I sat down, wondering which of my many misdeeds he was about to deal with.

'Well Ian,' he began, 'your sentence will be over soon. We have been in discussion and have a proposal to make. You are due some remission on the sentence, and you can have it if you agree to live at your father's home rather than the place you were living prior to this sentence.'

I was flabbergasted. I had not heard from my Dad for a long time. When I left Gran's, communication with the family dropped off a bit. I occasionally saw Gran in the town, and very infrequently I would call at the house – usually when I was desperate for some money. She would usually mention what Dad was up to, but I had not spoken to him directly for years. I knew that his relationship with Mary was over and that he had recently taken up with someone else. It was hard to believe that he had offered, or at least, agreed, to have me to live with them. It had to be worth a try, especially if it got me out of prison early.

'OK, then. If it's all right with my Dad, I'll go there.'

'Great,' said the probation officer, 'I'll set things in motion.' He looked at me seriously. 'This is a chance for you to get your life back on track, Ian, away from bad influences. Don't blow it.'

I nodded and grunted. I was used to hearing little lectures like that, but he did have a point. Maybe I would give it a try.

For a while, I did give it a try. It was strange being back with my Dad again. I got on well with his new partner, Joan, who was caring and non-judgemental. I always sensed that she understood me, but even so, I was not prepared to lower my defences. They had both obviously decided to try and help me rehabilitate.

I managed to stay out of trouble over the next few months, though I didn't stop my drinking or drug-taking. Gradually, though, I became restless and despondent. I was grateful to Dad for letting me live with him, but I struggled in my relationship with him. We didn't actually row much, but there was no depth – hardly surprising since we hardly knew each other.

I also felt increasingly disillusioned at the way the world was going. Global disasters like famine, war and pollution left me feeling impotent and disgusted. I didn't want to be part of a society that was ruining itself in such a way. I could see no hope for the future, and I didn't like what I saw in the present. My only means of dealing with such emotions was to escape into the oblivion created by alcohol and drugs. It was not long before all my old habits took over again.

The need for drugs overrode all sense of logic and common sense. One night, I broke into a chemist's shop, intent on stealing their drugs supply. Having entered the shop, I quickly realised that all the dangerous drugs were in the safe, and that accessing it would involve moving a large filing cabinet that was blocking my way. This was the point at which I should have decided to call off the whole idea and slide silently out of the shop. But I was too desperate to think straight, and continued with the break-in.

The room containing the safe was very small, and having tugged and shoved for some considerable time, I managed to slide the cabinet to one side, only for it to topple over. It was now wedged above me. I was trapped, about to become the only burglar in history to be caught next to his haul, unable to touch it. I was determined that this would not be the case, and with superhuman strength, pushed and heaved the filing cabinet, somehow managing to shift it sufficiently to crawl free. Even then, I didn't call it a day. Having made the safe accessible, I broke into it and found a collection of Class A drugs, including heroin and cocaine.

The next three weeks were a haze of highs, as I, with some of my friends, went on a binge to dispose of my booty. I don't know whether I went to work or not, but if I did, I wouldn't have been much use. I have vague memories of going to a club during this time, high on cocaine and full of confidence, and relieving myself on a police van parked outside. A policeman came round the side and saw me, but I appeared so self-assured and in control, that he left me to it without saying a word. I felt untouchable! This proved to be short-lived.

Early one morning, I was wrenched from a heavy, drug-induced sleep by a loud banging on the door. Before I had properly awoken, there was the sound of footsteps on the stairs, and brusque voices ordering my Dad and Joan out of bed. I could hear Joan crying and Dad shouting angrily. Then there was thumping and banging as doors were opened, cupboards emptied and floorboards taken up. I wondered briefly about making a run for it, but my brain and body were functioning far too slowly. Even as the thought passed through my mind, there were policemen in the room, searching everything. I stared in silence. I could think of nothing to say.

The search didn't take very long. Soon, the police had a pile of items in plastic bags, including an empty cocaine bottle. I was allowed to get dressed, and then was immediately arrested and taken to the police van. My Dad was furiously upset. His concern seemed to be more for the distress Joan had suffered and the humiliation they would undergo, rather than for me. I apologised as I went out of the door knowing that this time, the situation was extremely serious.

Which is how I came to be in this cell now, pondering my memories and fighting against the emotions they evoke. When I first came in, before the trial, my fellow prisoners, not endowed with sensitivity, told me I was looking at 15 years at least. The thought of spending so long behind bars was appalling. I didn't know whether I could bear it. Waiting for the trial with so much uncertainty, was agonising. I could do nothing but mope in my cell, not wanting to socialise or even eat. I was well-known in the prison because my arrest had been front-page news and had even made local television.

Everybody, therefore, felt obliged to talk to me and give an opinion on my case. I began to get seriously depressed and was given medication to treat the symptoms.

Only two things kept me going during this dreadful waiting period. One was the fact that a good friend was also inside, serving a three-month sentence. He spent a lot of time with me, trying to cheer me up and encourage me. The other was the motivating feeling of revenge. The person who had informed on me to the police and thus got me into this situation was also inside. I was incensed that he had been put on the same wing, but saw it as an opportunity for revenge. Obviously, I was not going to get directly involved with any reprisals, as this would be added to any sentencing at the trial, but there were many people around me who would act on my behalf. I kept my depression at bay by plotting all sorts of nasty scenarios for this former 'mate'. Eventually, though, word must have leaked out somehow, because he was placed on protection before anything happened to him.

The trial day came and inwardly I was a shaking mass of emotions. Outwardly, I was curt and irritable. Part of me was almost relieved that the uncertainty was over, even though I was expecting the worst – 15 years. Part of me was terrified at the prospect, unable to believe that this could be happening to me, wanting the comfort of a relative or friend to stand by me.

The judge had a bad reputation among the criminal population. He was South African and rumour had it that over there he had sent people to be hanged. I was not as fazed by such stories as I might have been, because I had been before him on more than one occasion, and had always found him fair. The court went through its ritual, and almost immediately after my letter of remorse was read out, I was being sentenced. There was an array of charges, and each one was getting three years. Numbly, I listened, mentally totting up the years. It was at least 15! I almost fainted with the shock, and was dimly aware of a hand on my shoulder, leading me back to the cells. Later, having returned to prison, I sat on my bed, paralysed by grief and fear. There was a knock on the door, and my lawyer walked in, smiling. I looked at him glumly. It was all right for him to smile; he didn't face the prospect of at least the next ten years behind bars, confined and claustrophobic.

'Well, that wasn't a bad verdict, all things considered,' he said briskly.

I stared at him. 'What do you mean? It seems pretty bad from where I'm sitting.'

The lawyer looked puzzled. 'You've got three years. All the sentences are to be served concurrently. You could be out in about two if you keep your nose clean.'

'Three years!!' I wanted to kiss him! I leapt to my feet with a victory salute, possibly the only man to rejoice over a three-year sentence.

Throughout the evening, various mates came to console me about my sentence, but I knew I'd had a lucky escape. I took a long look at my present situation and realised that I had three options. The first was to continue deeper and deeper into depression, allowing all the hateful things about prison life to disturb and destroy me. I could well imagine that this route could lead to suicidal feelings; I had been close to those already. The second option was to rebel against the authority that had put me here, by complaining, making trouble and causing problems whenever I could. I had seen quite a lot of people choose this option and end up at a definite disadvantage. The third option was to accept the

CHAPTER FOUR
Escape with a difference

I peered round the side of the farm building, looking cautiously in every direction. There was no one to be seen, though I could hear people talking and laughing quite nearby. It was the lunch break, and we were allowed a bit of time to ourselves. Most of the lads were playing a game of football, while others sloped off to have a walk and a smoke. I could hear the car engine turning over in the adjoining lane. Cautiously, I motioned to my two mates. 'Get in there now. There's nobody about. If I'm not back in 30 minutes, go back to the van. Just keep out of sight till then.' Grinning, and clutching the cigarettes I'd given them as payment, they scuttled into the barn, looking forward to a rest and a quiet smoke. I just hoped they wouldn't set the barn alight while they were about it. With another furtive glance around, I made a dash for the waiting car, flung myself in the back and burrowed under the blanket.

I had spent months planning this little escapade, considering meticulously every little detail. I had now been in prison long enough to be allowed on outside work parties. Every morning, a whole group of us were driven to a nearby farm. Ironically, this farm had been used as an internment camp during the Second World War, for all the Germans, Italians and other 'aliens' who were deemed to be a threat to national security. Most of these internees were businessmen, such as restaurant owners and their families who were living and working in Britain at the outbreak of war. In fact, many farms on the island were used in this way, with this particular farm in Patrick holding the largest group of about forty thousand prisoners.

When I discovered all this history, it added to the irony of the situation, as I had been given a German nickname – Rayner Bonhoff – when I was 11. This was the name of a West German footballer, though I don't think it was my footballing skills as much as my surname which acquired me the nickname! (I only played for the town side twice, that was Peel AFC, and we lost both times, not helped by me disappearing at half-time to find a cigarette!) It appealed to my somewhat sardonic sense of humour that, having had no escapes from the place when it was an internment camp, I was now attempting one, complete with German name! This historical context also heightened my sense of daring and adventure. I felt as if I was starring in a remake of *The Great Escape*!

We were given various manual duties to keep us busy and useful. Seeing an opportunity I volunteered to be work party chef, which meant I returned to the barns 30 minutes early to prepare the meal. I could eat my lunch as I worked, which gave me a whole hour free while the others were eating. I had chosen this particular day because the officer in charge was a more relaxed, less suspicious person. I was fairly sure that he wouldn't come looking for me for some time.

The car sped off from the farm. No one saw us go. Both Tom (the driver) and myself were laughing a bit manically, nerves and excitement combining to make us rather hysterical. 'Get a grip,' I whispered to my mate. 'People'll think you're mad, laughing to yourself like that.' This was home territory, and I had to stay hidden in case someone recognised me. My heart was racing and the adrenalin was pumping round my system. Fear and exhilaration rushed through me in equal measures. Every time we came to a stop at a junction, my heart gave a lurch, wondering if we'd been discovered. But so far, so good.

We were soon at our destination, a nondescript semi on an estate. Tom parked up swiftly and I jumped out, turning up my jacket collar, in a somewhat vain attempt to disguise my identity. I pressed my finger on the bell and kept it there until its irate owner flung the door open.

'What the hell are you playing ...' he started and then his face changed as he recognised me. 'What the f*** are you doing here? I thought you'd got three years!'

'Nice way to welcome an old friend,' I drawled, sounding calmer than I felt.

'B***** h***, mate, come in out of the way,' he said. 'Are you on the run? Cos if so, I can't ...'

I cut him off before he embarrassed himself. 'It's OK, mate, I'll be away in a minute. You haven't seen me, right? Just give me some drink and tobacco and hurry up about it.' When I'd got what I wanted, I ran back to the car, dived under the blanket and told Tom to step on it, just like they do in the films. We had quarter of an hour left.

However, unlike the films, the car did not accelerate off with a screech of tyres. It wouldn't start! I began to panic, my already fast breathing increasing to almost hyperventilation. Why, at this vital moment, wouldn't it start? We were on a hill, so Tom got the car rolling, intending to jump-start it. I could hardly hear the engine over the pounding of my heart. Twice the engine turned over, and twice it failed to start. My heart began to feel as if it was having the same problems.

'What the hell's the matter with it?' I muttered from under the blanket.

'Beats me,' growled Tom. 'You're gonna have to push in a minute.'

'Don't be stupid. I might be seen! This is Peel – everybody knows everybody. They say if you tell somebody something at the top of the shopping street, by the time you've reached the bottom, somebody else is telling you your business. That's how fast gossip travels in this place.'

'Well, it's a better risk than sitting in a car that won't go, or going on the run.'

He was right. I didn't want to have to spend the rest of my life looking over my shoulder, or get caught and spend even longer inside. This escape was only supposed to be very temporary. I cursed under my breath and tried to calm down. There was still a way to go before the hill flattened out. The car jolted its way down, coughing and spluttering but never quite firing. Just as I was giving up hope and wondering what on earth to do next, the car gave another cough and the engine caught. 'Thank God for that,' I breathed. 'C'mon Tom, let's get this clapped-out old thing back before it dies on us completely.' Tom grunted, a bit offended, but put his foot on the accelerator and we rushed along the narrow roads, still a bit shaky from the scare we'd had. I needed something strong to fortify me after that!

About half a mile from the farm, Tom pulled to a stop and glanced up and down the road. 'All clear!' he said. 'You'd better get going fast.'

'Thanks, mate,' I said, 'I'll see you right when I get out. Cheers!'

Tom smiled and nodded and put the car into gear as I slammed the door and ran towards the hedge. I skirted round two fields, keeping low and nearly tearing my hands on brambles. What an adventure! I felt high with elation and excitement, even though I was going back towards captivity. My two mates, who had been acting as a type of insurance cover for me, were still propped up against a hay bale when I finally puffed back in. (No one would think I was seriously missing if I was with them, because they were only a few weeks away from release and would not jeopardise that by doing a runner.) They looked impressed.

'Have you really been out and into town,' said one, disbelievingly.

I nodded, showing them the proof. 'And we've even got time for a drink before we start back.'

Laughing with the sheer fun of it all, I joined them against the hay bale.

Having adventures had always been an important part of my life, so it was hardly surprising that I had just completed such a crazy one. The need for thrills and excitement had relentlessly driven me, not only towards drink and drugs, but also to wild, sometimes dangerous activities.

Nearly every weekend when I wasn't in prison, a whole crowd of us would travel around the island, camping out or sleeping in vans, drinking, taking drugs and generally having a party. One evening, having set up camp, several of us went to a nearby pub called the Tholt-y-will to top up our drinks supply. On the way back, we took a warning flashlight from some roadworks and put it on top of the van. As we neared the camp, we could see the rest of our mates scurrying round the fire in panic, obviously thinking we were the police. When they realised their mistake, they were furious, having just thrown vast quantities of pot on the fire.

We finally settled down, and crashed-out in the van to sleep off the effects of our drinking and 'magic mushrooms', only to be woken early in the morning by a loud banging. Peering out, we saw it was the police. We quickly barred the door and refused to come out. We had a large vicious Alsatian that would deter most people! They said they wanted to question us about a robbery in a local pub. We hadn't committed it, but had no wish to go through tedious police procedure while they found the truth, so we stayed put, laughing at our ability to outwit them. It would have meant 48 hours in a police cell.

Then to our horror, we heard the van starting up. I had left the keys in the ignition, and two policemen had jumped into the front seat and were driving us to the Station. I stuck my head through the connecting window and yelled at them to stop. When they ignored me, we tried a different tactic, namely rocking the van from side to side as we drove along. At one point, just as we were going down a narrow lane with a 20-foot drop on one side, we managed to make the van rock onto two wheels. It came to an abrupt stop soon afterwards and a shaken police officer got out. After more shouting through the door, we finally got out and I, as the one fitting a description of the robber, agreed to go down to the Police Station the next day with my lawyer. Thankfully the incident fizzled out when the real culprits were arrested soon afterwards.

Another great adventure was the Glastonbury Kipper Scheme. A friend had some old film from a chemist's stockroom, which another friend in Lancaster offered to swap for a load of kippers. For some reason, this appealed to me as a great idea, and eight of us hired a van to take these kippers to the famous music festival in Glastonbury. The idea was that we would sell the kippers and thus fund our 'living expenses' at the festival. I thought that kippers would be a huge attraction to the 'alternative' hippies who frequent Glastonbury. Also, I didn't think anyone else would be selling them, so giving us a niche market. We set off from Lancaster in our hired van with eight boxes, each containing 100 kippers. It was a hot summer that year, and even before we had completed the journey, the van was beginning to smell.

We gave two hippies a lift on the last leg of the journey. They already had wristbands giving them access to the festival, so we all hid in the back of the van as we went through the gate so that we didn't have to pay.

Having set up camp and indulged in some drink and drugs, we decided that we had better open our kipper shop. Of course, we hadn't brought any equipment or advertising materials, so in the end, our stall was a hole in the ground with a barbed wire grill. We started cooking, but got no customers at all. There was nothing else for it; we had to drum up some interest. So, while some of us kept cooking, my friend and I walked around the site shouting 'Kippers for Trippers!' and 'Trippers, come and get your kippers!' This did have some limited success, and we managed to sell quite a few fish to some very weird people. By the end of our stay, having eaten kippers for every meal, and having given loads away, we still had three boxes left. By this time, we were fairly oozing kipper juice. Our clothes reeked of it, and naturally we didn't have anything clean to change into.

This didn't dampen my adventurous spirit, however, and, with a friend, I took a ferry to Holland, intent on visiting that drugs mecca, Amsterdam. We were very short of money, due to our failed kipper venture, and so had to jump trains. This was where the rank odour of kipper came to our aid. We stank so much that everyone avoided us and didn't bother to check whether we had paid. We had to sleep out overnight, and were rescued by a kindly American, who took us to a coffee shop, where we got warm and stoned. It was a hard job, hitching all the way back to the Isle of Man, but we managed it. I was very glad to get back to a bath and a clean set of clothes, and even more pleased that I had survived such an exhilarating exploit. For me at that time, such adventures made living worthwhile, which was why I felt impelled to carry on with them, even when inside.

Prison life had its highs and lows, though most of the time it was just monotonous. Sometimes, the frustration got too much and I felt very depressed again. When I was a child, they said I'd end up inside if I wasn't careful, but I didn't believe them. I was too absorbed in the present to think about the future. Besides, I thought I would stay lucky. One thing led to another, and I never stopped to reflect upon the way my life was going. I became a criminal without really noticing.

I hated life inside. Some people say you get used to it, but I never did. I hated the claustrophobic feeling of being shut in all the time. I hated the routine and the restrictions, the atmosphere of aggression and intimidation. I longed to get out, and resented every moment spent cooped up in the small, dreary cell.

To try and block out such feelings, I would do anything to help the time pass more quickly. I continued with exercise and weight training, and, of course, my studies. Some of my other activities were not so commendable though. One day, a few of us managed to concoct some hooch, with ingredients filched from the kitchens and smuggled into the dormitory in plastic bags. That night we had a great party. Ignoring pleas from other dormitories (which were hooch-less!) we got totally drunk and sang deafeningly and discordantly until the early hours. The next morning (fortunately a Sunday), we all felt extremely ill. No one seemed at all sympathetic to our pale faces and life-threatening headaches, including the medical officer, who refused our request for a paracetamol with a brusque obscenity.

Some time later, the boredom and frustration became too much for me again, and I decided that I wanted a change of scene. By this time I was in a single cell, which probably added to my loneliness and boredom, but which did help my cunning plan. Soon after lights out one night, I jumped off my bed, landing as loudly as I could, and then lay on the floor and banged on the door. I couldn't ring the bell as this was about four feet off the floor, and I wanted to act very injured. I was only wearing boxer shorts and the cell floor was cold. I banged harder on the door, hoping the guard wouldn't take too long to arrive. When he did, I deployed my best acting skills, groaning and moaning about my back. I gasped in pain as he prodded me.

'Fell off the top bunk ... can't move.' He looked a bit dubious, but told me to stay still while he went to get an ambulance. I was shivering already, and by the time (20 minutes later) the paramedics arrived, I was shaking and nearly blue.

'Shock,' said one, as he took my pulse. The other one nodded.

'Better get him in straightaway, something could be broken.' They strapped me up securely and trundled me off to the local hospital.

My acting skills were tested to the limit over the next few hours. Part of me was longing to laugh, while the rest struggled to remember to wince and groan at appropriate times. After a while though, a more urgent problem surfaced; I was bursting for the loo. The nurse promised to help me and then disappeared. When she finally returned, it was with an odd shaped container.

'No, of course you can't get out of bed to the loo,' she snapped in reply to my plea. 'You mustn't even move your arms. You'll have to use this.'

It was the most embarrassing pee of my life. A disgusted-looking prison officer held the bottle while I performed, practically overfilling it in the process.

Several examinations and an X-ray later, I was pronounced ready to return to the prison. This was bad news. I had planned on at least a few days in hospital. The good news, though, was that I had to have a week in bed, to allow my injury to heal. The authorities kindly put me in with an old friend – someone I had grown up with – to look after me. He played along with the hoax admirably and waited on me hand and foot for a week, bringing me food, magazines, tapes and washing gear, and helping me to the loo. After the evening check at eight o'clock, he would put tissue over the spy hole so that I could get up and exercise. Any more than a week, and the joke would have worn too thin for him; I couldn't resist calling him Jeeves or Florence Nightingale, and though it got him out of other duties, he was beginning to tire of doing all the work while I lay back and enjoyed the pampering. The whole wing was in on the deception, and various inmates used to pop their heads round the door to ask solicitously after my health.

After a few days of this, the Governor came round to see how I was. Wincing and smiling bravely, I asked if he would consider reducing my sentence by a few weeks, so that I could be out for my 21st birthday. The Governor was a reasonable man, whose compassion had not been hardened into cynicism. He was nearing the end of his term of office, and had already reduced some prisoners' sentences. After some thought and consultation, he sent word that he would grant my request. I was overjoyed, and made a seemingly miraculous recovery soon afterwards. Some of the prison officers, who maybe had reason to be cynical, watched contemptuously as I ran round the exercise yard within a few days.

It was the best day of my adult life so far. The door opened in the big gates and I stepped through to freedom. I had never appreciated what being free was before, but now, after two years without it, I was ecstatic. I walked a few steps and breathed deeply. At last! There was no one there to greet me and welcome me back to the outside world, so I shouldered my bag and strode towards the bus stop.

As I paused at the kerb to cross the road, I was shocked by how busy it was. The constant traffic, with its noise and speed, completely overwhelmed me. I hadn't realised how much I had been removed from the bustle of ordinary life. For two years, I had kept to imposed routines and spent much of my time in a small room. Even though I had been in prison before, it had not been for such a long time, and I had not anticipated what a shock it would be to come out again.

True to form though, I didn't take long to get over the shock. I embarked on what seemed like a six-month party to celebrate my release. I had gained quite a reputation on the island which stood me in good stead in criminal circles. I found that I had instant access to a way of life that was immensely attractive. I had status and respect, and soon I began to gain the trappings of wealth. My stint in prison had not deterred me from a drug-using, criminal lifestyle. Within a very short space of time, I was drinking heavily and regularly using all sorts of drugs.

Life got even better when I fell in love – not that I realised it at first, because I wasn't sure what love was. I'd had girlfriends before but nothing serious. Then I started going out with Jess, a girl I had known since school days. I was besotted. She was everything I had dreamt of; fun, kind and good-looking – and she liked me.

We had been going out for only a few weeks when we decided to move in together. At the time, Jess was sharing a large house with eight other girls and one bloke. They were all professionals; different from the people I'd shared a dorm with in prison. We shared one of the small rooms in the house, and I often felt as if I was hiding in there from the rest of the household as I struggled to connect with them on their level – not so much because they were more educated than me, but because they were all from nice homes and didn't seem to have had any great struggles in life. They all seemed pretty secure in themselves and didn't need drugs to cope in a social setting. It highlighted, uncomfortably, my own insecurity. I remember one day when ten of my best hippy-looking friends turned up in their VW pick-up to go out on one of our adventures. Their arrival didn't seem to be appreciated by my house mates.

I was trying desperately to fit in and I felt torn between two worlds. Jess was also feeling the pressure, so we decided to look for our own place together. After a bit of searching, we managed to find a small terraced one-bedroom cottage to rent in Douglas. It was perfect; all my dreams were coming true. We decided that it was too soon to start a family, but instead got a cat and a dog, a much easier (and, with hindsight, wiser) option! We called the cat Ginny, after a witch who lived at the top of our street, and the dog Marley, after the famous Bob. They gave us hours of entertainment, chasing each other across the backs of the chairs and the settee, then up the stairs, thundering across the bedroom, only to come hurtling once more down the stairs. I remember waking one morning, after Jess had gone to work, to find Marley under the covers with his head on the pillow, while Ginny lay on the other side, doing the same. I could hardly get out of bed, I was laughing so much.

Life was good. I decided to go self-employed rather than seek work elsewhere, as I wanted to put the profit into my own pocket instead of someone else's. I thought I would give the building trade a try as I had friends who could do most jobs in that area, and I did have some limited success. The peak of my building career was a big job renovating the outside of a hotel on the opposite side of the island in Ramsey. Even this turned into an adventure, as I persuaded the owner to let us stay in one of the hotel rooms so that we could be on the job early each morning. This proved to be a big mistake on his part. We got an advance on our living expenses for each day of the job, and used it getting extremely drunk and stoned each night. The result was that we didn't start work any earlier than we might have done if we'd stayed at home. We did however manage to complete the job (a minor miracle!), though by the time we'd had all our advances, there were no wages left.

I then tried my hand at logging and found a barn to operate from. I hadn't really done any preparatory thinking or planning, which meant that I made a lot of very hard work for my assistant, Chris, and myself.

One day, while using the chainsaw, Chris kept pestering me to let him have a go, so I reluctantly agreed. After a couple of minutes, disaster struck. The saw hit a knot in the wood, bounced up and cut into Chris's head, missing his eye by centimetres. It cut down to his skull and ran for about four inches up to the top of his head. He turned to face me with a big gormless smile and said, 'I'm cut.' I was nearly sick. I quickly pulled myself together so as not to show him the severity of the incident and so shock him. Hastily, I found an old T-shirt in the van, wrapped it tightly round his head, and got him to hold his brains in while we sped off to hospital. Fortunately, the injury was not as serious as it might have been, and after 11 stitches, he was sent home to recover. This proved to be the end of my logging exploits.

As for the relationship, it still seemed to be going well – from my point of view. I was very selfish and didn't give a lot of consideration to Jess. She had quite a good job as a civil servant. I would stay up half the night drinking and smoking pot, trying to get her to do the same, never pausing to consider that she had to get up at eight o'clock each morning to go to work. Not only that, but she often came downstairs each morning to various unconscious people strewn across the living-room. Jess rarely complained and seemed most of the time to accept the lifestyle I had introduced her to. I couldn't believe that I had found someone so lovely.

But life was not as idyllic as I thought. The problem was that I wasn't allowing her to get anywhere near the real me. I couldn't pull down the barriers I'd spent years erecting to protect myself, and when Jess tried, it would often end in arguments and even, on a number of occasions, with me lashing out. I hated myself for this and it proved to be the final nail in the coffin of our relationship, together with the fact that we were in dire financial circumstances, as we had taken on a mortgage to buy our rented house.

When Jess told me it was over, I couldn't cope. Yet again I'd had everything taken away from me. That familiar feeling of my world falling apart returned once more, and I cried for days, weeks. Even years afterwards, I still found myself crying over my loss. It was worse than a bereavement in some ways, because it lacked the finality, the closure of death that can eventually bring healing.

That week was the worst of my life; worse even than when I was sent to prison. I hadn't realised just how much I loved Jess until she wasn't there. I wanted her back so badly that I ached. I wanted to tell her how sorry I was for hurting her, for being so selfish, but it was too late. The enormity of the way I had treated her fell on me like an avalanche. I felt as if I was suffocating under an unbearable weight. During that week I couldn't let her go. I would constantly ring her at work, until in the end she wouldn't take the calls. I haunted the friend's house where she was staying, kicking the door when she wouldn't let me see her. I even drove my van into her work's wall one day when I had to return it to be sold.

For once in my life I was face-to-face with the real me, and I didn't like what I saw. I had become totally self-centred, unable to express emotions, maybe even to feel them any more. I couldn't even connect with the person I thought I loved. I hadn't tried to understand her and had constantly kept her at arm's length. All she had wanted was to be close to me, to be part of my life and for me to be part of hers. I couldn't see beyond the physical fulfilment of my needs, whether that was sex, drink or drugs. She had given up so much for me, and I had taken her for granted – until now. Now I saw where I had been in the wrong. I realised that the lifestyle I had been pursuing had denied me the depth of relationship I truly wanted and needed.

I didn't think the situation could get any worse. I thought I was in the depths of despair. Then, some days after Jess had left, and I was still desperately trying to get her back, our dog, Marley, who was my constant companion, wandered across a quiet country road and was knocked over and killed. Somehow, the combination of these two shattering events was too much for me. My outer toughness, fragile at the best of times, crumbled. I couldn't stop crying or thinking about what I had lost. I didn't want to talk to anyone or go anywhere.

My friends, not normally bothered about anything except where their next 'fix' (be it drink, drugs or some other stimulation) was coming from, were quite concerned about me. I think they thought I was losing my sanity. One of them actually gave me £400 to 'go away and get my head sorted'. Numbly, not really knowing what I was doing, and not caring, I let them make some arrangements and went off to a small town in Lancashire for a few weeks. During that time, I squandered all the rest of the money on heroin, and spent the whole fortnight oblivious to my surroundings, in a narcotic stupor.

Finally, having run out of money, I went home, hoping against hope that in my absence, Jess might have had a change of heart and returned. She had not; there was no message, no letter, nothing. I wanted to die. I left the house, unable to cope without her and the dog, and went to stay with a friend. Various mates visited to try and cheer me up, but I was in deep depression. Then, one evening, someone arrived with some more heroin. I took it, desperately wanting the dream-like state it brought, the escape from reality. With heroin, I could bury my head in the sand.

My head was to remain in the sand of heroin for the next six years. Six years that should have been the best years of my life, wasted in a cycle of highs and lows. Every time I came off the drug for a while, the memories and pain would come flooding back and so would the tears. I came to depend more and more on it, looking forward to the next fix, and hating the feeling when it began to wear off. I could not hold down a job for long, so yet again I was reliant on criminal activities to fund my habit.

After about three years of this bleak life, I met an attractive girl, quite a few years younger than me, who seemed to like me a lot. We started going out, and I wondered whether this might be a turning point in my condition. Lisa was a bright girl, just about to go to university, who was enjoying being a bit more independent and daring. She obviously relished the idea of going out with an 'older man' and was excited by my slightly dangerous reputation. No doubt her parents were horrified, which perhaps was part of the attraction.

It didn't take long to discover that much as I liked Lisa, and enjoyed her company, I didn't, and probably couldn't love her. I was still obsessed with Jess, and couldn't accept that anyone could replace her. Yet even knowing this, I still carried on going out with Lisa. I liked having someone special; it kept the demon loneliness at bay. I think she realised that something was missing from the relationship, but she didn't give up on it. I remembered all my regrets when Jess left, and my realisation then of my inadequacy in the relationship, but I still continued to make the same mistakes with Lisa. I didn't care enough to make the effort. If she was happy to put up with things the way they were, that was fine. And if she wasn't, well, she knew what she could do about it. I would miss her, but I wouldn't be devastated.

Lisa dabbled on the edge of the drugs scene. She was not as seriously involved as I was, but could not avoid being part of it to some extent. One day, after we had been going out for about a year, there was a drugs raid on my flat. Not much was found, as I was always careful, except for a small amount of pot in Lisa's coat. She was not even in the flat, but had left her coat behind. I told the police that the drug was mine, and they were prepared to believe me. I was arrested and locked up overnight. The following day, I was taken to the small town of Ramsey some miles away, where a court was opened up specially to try and sentence me. When Lisa heard that I'd been given three months, she felt both guilty and grateful. In a strange way, I had managed to add something valuable to the relationship and so extend its natural course. She thought I'd been extremely unselfish and sacrificial in protecting her, and revised what had become a somewhat low opinion of me.

Soon after I was released, however, Lisa left the Isle of Man to go to university in Leeds. I had been feeling for some time that the island was getting a bit small to contain me. The police were keeping a close eye on me, and I knew that it would only be a matter of time before I was arrested again. It didn't occur to me that an alternative was to go straight. Instead, I began to think more and more seriously about joining Lisa in Leeds.

I didn't really want to live in a city. I was used to living in the countryside, and felt restricted and claustrophobic in the noise and dirt of a big city. Another concern was that I knew my heroin addiction would increase. Heroin was more readily available and cheaper in England, and I knew I would give in to such temptation. But, on further reflection, I decided that this ready availability was a positive reason to go. After all, I was sometimes beginning to need more heroin than I could easily obtain.

Eventually, circumstances helped me to make the decision. The police caught up with me regarding an unpaid fine of £450. Lisa generously gave me half of it, and I raised the other half by fraudulently selling a car I no longer owned to a mate. He paid me on the strength of the log book and my assurance that it was still in the long stay car park at the airport, where I had been unable to get it out due to lack of money. I knew I would need to make myself scarce when he discovered the truth o the matter. Then I broke my ankle while playing football, which meant that I was not very mobile, should my former mate come looking for me. It was time to leave the Isle of Man. Within a few days, complete with crutches, a couple of bags and a new dog, Ziggy, I arrived in Leeds.

CHAPTER FIVE
A Leeds beggar

Leeds – a great sprawling mass of houses and tower blocks thrusting out into the surrounding hills and moors. Constant noise from traffic that alternately speeds and crawls through every street. Fumes and fog clog the air, suffocating. People hurry and jostle, bustle and force their way through the days, always looking somewhere else. I alone stand still, besieged by shabby buildings, smelly ginnels, dirty, litter-strewn pavements.

It was an alien and hostile world to come into. I missed the open spaces and wild, clean beauty of the Isle of Man. Most of all I missed the sea. As for everyone who has lived near the sea, its vastness and rhythm had become part of my life. I didn't belong here, but I had little choice. It was a new start, and I came with every intention of making the most of it. Lisa was enjoying university, and didn't want the problems she had encountered with me before. I agreed to do my best.

My best lasted precisely one day; the length of time it took me to get the dog and me settled into our new abode. After that, the yearning for heroin was too strong to resist. My only contact for the drug at that time was a mate in Manchester, so I started taking regular trips over the Pennines. It was costly, and I didn't have a job, so borrowed from Lisa, though she grew increasingly reluctant to lend me any money. She saw the effect that the drugs were having on me, and on our relationship, and she became more and more hostile to what I was doing. The tension between us intensified.

One day, not wanting to provoke another argument, I stole Lisa's credit card, discovered her pin number and took £300 out of her account. Did I think it was stealing? I didn't really think about it at all. It was a means of getting what I needed, and I guess I thought she would come round eventually. I went to stay at my mate's place, and got totally stoned, spending the entire amount in a week. When the drugs ran out, I finally came round enough to shamble back to Lisa's. I thought she would probably have my bags packed and Ziggy on a lead, but to my surprise, after shouting at me for a while, she gave me another chance with the ultimatum that I choose her or the drugs.

Of course, I chose her, but she should have known better. Even as I was saying the words, I knew they were empty. I had to back up my lies with deceit, and started hiding my drugs from her, using them when she wasn't around to see the effects. I discovered that there was a small gap above the door frame in the bathroom, which was just the right size for my purposes. Lisa was quite small, and so would never notice.

I was right; she didn't notice, until the time, when, desperate for a fix, I forgot to lock the bathroom door. Unaware that I was in there, she walked in. Immediately, she saw what I was doing and her face screwed up in shock and disgust. 'I might have known I couldn't trust you,' she shouted. 'Ian how **could** you?'

Her reproachful look was hard to bear. I concentrated on finishing the task in hand and then said, speech bit slurred, 'I'm sorry. It was only this once.'

'Don't give me that,' she snapped, 'I don't believe you. I thought we had something going, but all you really care about is killing yourself.' She fairly spat out the last two words, and then stormed down the stairs, slamming the living-room door. There was no point in following her. I went to the bedroom to allow the drug to take effect.

The relationship was finished. I'd known it for a long time really, and I think she had too. I'd never really loved her, though I'd enjoyed being with her until she started nagging me about the drugs. She fulfilled my needs on an emotional as well as a physical level. I never thought whether I fulfilled hers. I should have gone before and let her get on with her life, but I needed someone to be around. I didn't like my own company. Now, though, there was no choice. If I stayed, the rows would increase, I would probably take even more drugs and get into trouble, and Lisa would wreck any chance she might have of getting her degree. In fact, any chance she might have of true happiness. I decided to go, before she threw me out.

Though I didn't love her and I was tired of her constant criticisms, I still felt desolate when I left. Lisa was crying, but made no effort to stop me. She knew it was the end. I waved as I walked away, Ziggy trotting at my heels. Inside, the familiar hard lump of pain and loneliness gnawed at me.

I had no idea where to go next. What I really wanted was to go back to the Isle of Man, but I knew I had destroyed any chance of returning there. There was no one I could turn to in this intimidating city. I was completely alone.

I wandered into the city centre, aimlessly looking into shops at goods I couldn't afford to buy. All my money had gone on drugs. It seemed I was going to have to revert to shoplifting in order to survive. It was not what I wanted. The danger of another prison sentence was too great. I couldn't face it. Also, I now had Ziggy to consider. He relied on me for everything, including affection, and I couldn't leave him alone. So, there had to be some other way.

As I wandered along, I noticed two men sitting on coats in a doorway, begging. With nothing better to do, I went to chat to them, even though I didn't have anything to give them. They seemed to recognise in me one of their own fraternity, and were friendly and welcoming. I stayed quite a long time with them, asking them about their lives, and telling them about my own situation. I noticed that they appeared to be acquiring quite a bit of money from passers-by.

Chris and John were good-natured guys. They didn't seem to mind me hanging around with them, and even sent me off with some of their 'earnings' to get sandwiches for us all. When they discovered that I was homeless, they offered me a place in their squat. As this included a bed and electricity, I accepted eagerly. I didn't want to be curling up with Ziggy on a park bench that night!

The more I spoke to my new friends, the keener I became on the idea of trying begging as a means of income. It seemed a reasonably effortless but potentially lucrative alternative to trying to find work or to criminal activities. So, the very next day, having laid claim to the spare bed and taken advice from Chris and John, I marched off to Safeway, the faithful Ziggy at my heels. I had brought an old blanket for us to sit on and a plastic container for the money. I set myself up, and sat down to wait.

It was not as easy as I had imagined. For a start, I had not reckoned on the total embarrassment and humiliation I would experience. I sat, not daring to look up, feeling like the lowest of the low, a piece of excrement on the pavement, to be hurriedly avoided. I could hardly believe that I had been reduced to begging, like some old tramp. I imagined how I would feel if my younger brother, Joey, were to see me now, or worse, my Gran. What would she say if she saw her beloved grandson, whom she brought up as her own child, begging on the street? Wave after wave of shame swept over me, and I began to feel very depressed, particularly as no one had given me a penny in two hours. I was such a failure I couldn't even beg!

When the daily sensation of drug withdrawal began, I got desperate, and plucked up the courage to ask a passer-by for some change. She walked past without a second glance. Then a woman heading for the supermarket door noticed the dog, sitting patiently next to me. Whether Ziggy's border collie, doleful brown eyes tugged at this shopper's heartstrings I shall never know, but she stopped and threw some money into my container with a smile. It was the breakthrough moment. After that, the money came steadily and by the time I was ready to go back to the squat, I had received enough for my fix and a tin of dog food.

It was never again as hard as on that first day. I don't know what made the difference, but over the next few weeks I gradually built up an income that was regularly between £60 and £80 a day. Perhaps it was because I no longer felt awkward and ashamed sitting there. It became quite normal. Also, people came to recognise me and maybe felt more obliged to give to me. It's harder to ignore someone that you know you're going to see again. I was always pleasant and thanked donors with a smile, which helped encourage them to give again.

They probably wouldn't have been as generous if they had known that nearly all my income went on drugs – mostly heroin, although I was also developing a taste for crack cocaine. I always made sure that there was enough to feed money Ziggy, but often I didn't leave enough to buy food for myself. The need for drugs was far more urgent than the need for food.

Once I felt established in my chosen 'career', I decided to fulfil a long-held ambition and grow my own cannabis. I set up a growing room in the squat with all the necessary equipment, including free electricity, and planted my first crop. After a few months, it was coming on nicely, and I was looking forward to harvest time. One morning, however, I was rudely awoken by the drug squad bursting in and arresting me. Apparently, the owners of the property had come into the house the previous day and discovered everything.

I had to go to court, and was expecting a very nasty fine, or worse, a prison sentence. I was therefore pleasantly surprised when I was fined £120. The sentence I had received for possessing a fraction of the amount of the drug on the Isle of Man was three months inside. However, I was not going to question the inconsistencies of our criminal justice system. I paid up meekly and got out quickly.

The incident left me without a home and without my crop. My most immediate problem was the urgent need to find new accommodation. It was nearly Christmas – not a good time to be homeless. Someone gave me the name of a landlord with property in Chapeltown, so I got in touch with him and arranged to go and look at a bedsit he had vacant. Chapeltown is considered by many to be one of the most run down, dangerous and needy areas of Leeds. I was too desperate to care and took the place.

My new home was a room in a house with seven other bedsits and one bathroom and toilet. My neighbours in the house were nearly all alcoholics, singing and shouting into every night, and fouling the bathroom with their failed efforts to make it to the toilet. The landlord didn't seem to care about the state of the house, or the bathroom in particular. His solution to the latter problem was to keep laying new bits of carpet, but without taking up the previous filthy, stinking layer. I referred to it as the bathroom's 'poo sandwich'. It became so revolting that in the end I couldn't go in there. I used to urinate out of my window onto the backyard, and use public toilets for all other needs.

Sometimes, I looked at myself and could hardly believe what I had become. My self-esteem, never really very buoyant, descended steadily as I normalised into an addicted beggar, shambling the streets and returning to a dirty, squalid cell of a room. How could I respect myself when no one else did? As always, my solution to such painful reflection was to lose myself in the comforting unconsciousness of drugs or drink. The barriers to feeling and vulnerability, built up since childhood, were at their strongest.

A typical day began at ten o'clock in the morning, when I struggled out of a drug-induced slumber and reached for my first fix. This had to be prepared the night before, because I always woke in the first stages of withdrawal, and could not get out of bed until I had injected myself. Having given myself the means to go on, I could then have breakfast and get dressed. My boots were so old and worn that they had huge holes in them, so I wore plastic bags between my socks and my boots. I never considered the irony of the fact that I was 'earning' nearly £500 per week, and yet could not afford to buy new boots.

Ziggy and I walked the two miles into the city centre. The dog was my saving grace. Without him, I think I might have finished it all at this time. He gave me something to live for, as well as being an affectionate and entertaining companion. Some people disapprove of beggars and homeless people having dogs, saying that it's cruel, and only a cynical way of claiming a bit more money. This may be true of a minority, but my experience is that for the majority in that situation, their dog is the only being in the world they can love, and who loves them. That was certainly my experience with Ziggy. He was my friend and I took good care of him.

We usually got to Safeway at about half past eleven, in time to catch the lunch-time rush. Because I was sitting down so much, I was permanently cold. My health was deteriorating and I frequently felt ill. I could only hope that the miserable, cold, ill figure I presented would touch people's heartstrings and encourage them to give. Ziggy, in contrast, kept on the move nearly all day, chasing pigeons, going up to greet and sometimes play with passers-by and sniffing at other dogs. He continued to use his soulful eyes and charming ways to increase the income. Everyone loved Ziggy. The only time I moved much was when I went to the nearby public toilets. Ziggy accompanied me there as well. He had learnt how to jump up to the sinks and drink from the taps.

I had many different responses to my presence near the supermarket. Some people speeded up when they spotted me sitting on my blanket near the entrance, so that they were practically running by the time they passed me. Others suddenly had a phone call, so that they could avoid seeing or hearing me. I particularly disliked the shoppers who looked so disgusted and disapproving as they glanced briefly at me. Nothing gave them the right to be so superior to someone in need. Sometimes, though not often, I did receive verbal abuse. Normally, I ignored it, though I was tempted to give as good as I got. Now and again, groups of children, egging each other on, showing off, would mock me, throwing pennies at me as they did so. I found that throwing them back, hard, usually got rid of them fairly quickly.

The begging day lasted until about seven o'clock in the evening, when most of the homeward traffic had died down and Safeway was closing. I gathered together all my money and went into the supermarket, to buy food for Ziggy and to change all the coins into notes. Safeway was very tolerant and accommodated me without complaint. I was never moved on from there, for which I was very grateful.

Every night, before I could head back to the bedsit, I had to score my drugs. Once I had got them, I made my way back as fast as I could. I was weary, though I hadn't had much exercise, but I needed to get back quickly because the sensations of withdrawal were beginning to take hold. First, though, I always fed the dog. I knew that he probably wouldn't get any food if I had my fix first. That done, I could inject the heroin and slump in front of the television for about four hours. I never knew what I was watching; mindless junk for a mindless viewer. Nothing mattered any more and I could forget the pain of everyday life for the evening.

It was a lonely, meaningless life. I had no real friends. My only contacts were a few fellow beggars and addicts. I hardly ever had a proper conversation with anyone. My whole focus was on getting enough money to be able to submerge myself in the illusion of escaping reality. In fact, the sensations following a drug fix **became** my reality. It was so-called 'normal' life that seemed unreal to me.

Even eating was a chore rather than a pleasure. I rarely felt hungry, and resented spending money on food; I needed it for drugs. Much of my food was donated by shoppers, who would buy me a sandwich or pasty as they went past. Occasionally I made a stew, on the little camping cooker that was all the cooking facilities I had. My meals were certainly not cordon bleu – despite my earlier experience as work party chef – but an unappetising combination of anything I could get cheap at the market. This I left on the hob, heating it up each day until I had finished it.

Each day blurred into the next, and it was only the changing seasons that gave me any clue that time was passing. I was in the prime of my life, yet I felt like a tired old man with little, if anything, to live for. Sometimes the pity of it threatened to overwhelm me, but with an instinct born out of long habit, I pushed such thoughts away.

Birthdays and Christmas caused an almost unbearable return of the emotions I was trying to deny. Though I knew deep down that no one was going to celebrate my birthday, there was still a glimmer of hope that somehow, someone would remember. I would sift through the pile of mail in the communal entrance hall, wondering if perhaps this time, someone might have found out where I was. But there was always nothing. With a mental shrug, and a bitter laugh at myself for being so optimistic, I would leave the house and walk to my pitch. The hard lump inside, growing like a cancer over the years since I first remember feeling it, made me want to gag. Another year past and nobody knew or cared.

Birthdays were only good for raising sympathy. As I called out to strangers passing by, I would say that it was my birthday, hoping that this would encourage them to give. Often, they did respond to the plea. So my birthday, no longer a cause for celebration, became corrupted into another cynical means of feeding my habit.

Christmas was an even worse time than my birthday. Even before I came to the streets of Leeds, I had disliked Christmas. From quite young, I had realised that somehow, something was missing from our version of this idealised time. I had liked getting presents, of course, although often, secretly, I was a bit disappointed with them. There was always the vain hope that something would come from my mother, and later, even my father wasn't around. My adoptive parents would not let us celebrate Christmas with our natural family, which always hurt.

As I grew older, and was more and more detached from any kind of family life, Christmas came to symbolise all that I had lost; a time when we were meant to be happily enjoying ourselves but were not.

One year, when I was sharing a flat with mates, a friend and I spent Christmas Day on our own. We had absolutely nothing to make it a special time; no presents, no food, no drink, no family, no celebration. It was a bleak, depressing day, highlighting how alone and desolate we really were.

Christmas was the time when I was faced with the hard reality of my situation; my piercing loneliness, self-enforced poverty, lack of freedom and love. By October in Leeds, the signs of Christmas were beginning to appear, and my heart sank. All around me, or so it seemed, people were happy, spending money on themselves and on one another, partying, spreading peace and good will.

On Christmas Day, I sat in my bedsit, in front of my £2 black and white television, watching the images of carefree fun and festivity. The contrast between what I saw on the screen, and my own awful situation was painfully poignant. I walked into town, maybe hoping to beg, maybe just to say 'Happy Christmas' to a living person, but the place was empty and silent, reflecting exactly my mood. Impulsively, I bought an Indian takeaway, and back at the bedsit, picked miserably at the unappetising contents before finally finding release in a dose of heroin.

Very occasionally, small events served to lighten the tedium and ache of daily life. Ziggy was usually the author of these. He was a playful dog, who found more of interest in each day than I did. He would wander a little way away from my pitch, but I never worried, because he knew exactly how far to go, and never strayed near traffic.

One day, he went to investigate something new on a neighbouring office block. Some ropes were dangling down the side of it, coming from a bosun's chair, strung 80 feet up in the air to enable the windows to be cleaned. Ziggy wasn't interested in why the ropes were there. He recognised their play potential. Within seconds, he had grabbed one of them in his mouth and was tugging and snarling, running round in circles, then letting go and grabbing the other one and repeating the process. Suddenly, there were loud shouts from above. Several people looked up to see a window cleaner clinging on to the bosun's chair as it flailed crazily around. Ziggy thought this was a great game, especially when I and some others joined in and tried to wrest the rope from him. Eventually, we succeeded and shouted apologies to the window cleaner, who replied with a good-natured salute. I had feared a bucketful of water on my head!

Sometimes, I had to act as if I didn't know Ziggy at all. He was naturally playful, and could be quite boisterous. When he saw a young guy on crutches moving slowly towards him, he thought this was the signal for a great game. He raced up to him and began wrestling the crutches from him, knocking him over in the process. I looked across to where the poor man was sprawled in the street, saw that there were plenty of people helping him and decided that it was best to pretend the dog was nothing to do with me. Ziggy meanwhile, realising from all the shouting at him that no one else wanted to play, had slunk off into the crowd.

On another occasion, he showed criminal tendencies. A lady called Rose, who used to give quite regularly to me, put her bag down as she was talking to me. Ziggy trotted up, stuck his head in her bag and brought out a five-pound note. It wasn't the food he was probably looking for, but it was a good toy, and he ran off, the fiver fluttering in his mouth. Rose shouted after him and I whistled. Fortunately, he was obedient and returned to the whistle, still carrying the five-pound note! Another tug of war ensued to retrieve it, with both of us laughing so much that we nearly tore it. Still laughing as she finally put the note away again, Rose asked whether I had trained him to do that. I replied that he had taught himself on the job. It was good to share a joke with someone again. For a moment, I forgot who and what I was, and felt normal again. As she walked away, I felt lonelier than ever.

CHAPTER SIX
The Big Issue

The man standing outside the bookshop was a regular on the streets of Leeds. He was part of the growing begging community, so I knew him by sight and to pass the time of day with. As I approached him, though, I realised there was something different about him. He was not asking for people to 'spare a bit of change'. He was shouting. 'Big Issue! Get your Big Issue here! Help the homeless!' On the pavement next to him was a pile of magazines. Curious, I went over.

'What's this then mate?' I asked by way of greeting. 'Something with the Yorkshire Post?'

He grinned. 'Na. It's a new mag. Specially for the homeless. I reckon I'm on to a good thing. Big Issue! New magazine!'

A smartly dressed woman came over and bought one, then moments later, a young man in a baseball cap proffered his money with a smile. I was impressed and picked one up to have a look at it.

It turned out that the new magazine was the brainchild of Gordon Roddick, of the Body Shop, inspired by something similar in New York. The aim, according to the blurb, was to:

- enable homeless people to earn an income through self-help;
- invest profits to benefit homeless people;
- provide homeless people with a voice in the media;
- produce a quality magazine which interests and informs readers;
- provide an example of a socially responsible business.

This all sounded a bit sophisticated for me, but I liked the basic idea. I decided I wouldn't mind giving it a go. I just needed to be sure that it would pay enough.

It was necessary for me to make at least as much money as I was currently getting through begging, to feed my habit. Drugs had got a tight grip on me, and I was needing more and more in order to maintain the highs I so desperately longed for. I discovered that I could buy the magazines at 30p each, with a retail price of £1. This seemed a good profit margin, and the magazine itself was obviously a good product. I decided to go for it.

From the beginning, I preferred selling the Big Issue to begging. I felt that in doing this, I had a little more dignity. I was giving something as well as getting. I was a street trader. There were still people who stared at me with unconcealed contempt as they hurried on, and certain types, usually youths, who shouted at me to get a f****** job, but on the whole, I noticed a much better response among passers-by. Many would stop to chat, in a way that they wouldn't if I was begging. Part of this was because I was standing up. Sitting is a very subservient position on the street and people are not comfortable with it. Standing meant that I was meeting shoppers and office workers at their own level, with something of integrity to offer them. It felt good.

Soon, I had built up a reasonable customer base. I was one of the first to sell the Big Issue in Leeds, so I could trade on the novelty value, helped by the fact that there was not yet much competition. It was published weekly by this time, and many came specially each week to buy their copy. I quickly found that I was earning as much as I had been by begging. Every now and again, I recognised someone from my past. I always felt embarrassed to see anyone from the Isle of Man, and hoped that they wouldn't remember who I was. An exception was the time when I saw a local boy who had made good. Frank McGee was someone I knew reasonably well from the island. He was a lead player in a band, who had left to go to London and had gone on to appear in *Eastenders*. Any embarrassment I might have had was swallowed up in gleeful anticipation. At last, someone rich who knew and liked me! He stopped to chat for quite some time, but slightly guiltily admitted that he didn't have a lot of cash on him. He was genuine and I was grateful for the not inconsiderable amount he did leave with me.

Once a fortnight, on the day that I collected my dole money, I gave myself a day off. The dole, like my other income, was injected straight into my arm, a constant, greedy drain of resources, energy and life itself. In my more sober moments, I knew that this was a stupid way to live. At such moments, I truly wanted to be free of the stranglehold that the drugs had on me.

I enrolled for various methadone programmes. Methadone is a heroin substitute and a transition for coming off the drug altogether. To be accepted on the course, I had to agree to give a urine sample every week, to prove that I was not taking heroin. Despite my best efforts, I nearly always failed the urine test and consequently never stayed long on the programmes.

When I first went, I saw a drugs counsellor, who was supposed to advise and encourage me. I discovered, however, that this person, though he had good intentions, had no practical experience of drugs or coming off them. His closest encounter with the hard world of hard drugs was the odd spliff at university. He was telling me how to solve my problems out of a textbook. I lost respect for him – and for the whole system he represented. Besides, it was just too difficult to stop taking heroin. The desire to kick the habit was no match for the craving for a fix when the withdrawal symptoms began.

The methadone was no substitute really. One week, I saved it up, in order to experience a proper 'hit'. The need for satisfaction overrode all other considerations of safety or common sense. I was possessed by the need for drugs. So, one evening, before I was even home, I injected five days' worth of methadone, and it nearly killed me. I collapsed against a wall, and must have been there, unable to move or speak, for about three hours. No one came to see what was wrong or to send for an ambulance. I was just left there, part of the rubbish littering the streets of Leeds.

Eventually, I could move enough to crawl back to the bedsit, half a mile away. I managed to get up onto the bed and stayed there for the next two-and-a-half days, drifting in and out of consciousness. I felt as if I was paralysed from the waist down, but was in too confused and brain-changed a state to be scared about this. At one point, I came to a little, felt terrible and gave myself an injection of heroin, thinking this might help. It didn't, and I drifted off into more nightmares, images and weird physical and mental sensations. At last, on the third day, I began to recover, much to Ziggy's delight. He had been waiting anxiously, unfed and unable to get out, for his master to return to him.

When it was all over and I looked back on those few days, even I felt a bit scared, and realised that I'd had a narrow escape. I resolved to give the programme another proper try. Unfortunately, I failed again at the urine sample stage. This time, try as I would, I could not produce the required sample. I went to explain the problem to the workers, but they were quite firm; no urine, no methadone. I wanted that drug. It may not have been as effective, in my terms, as heroin, but nonetheless, I needed it at that moment. So I returned to the loos by way of the kitchen, collecting a small glass of orange juice as I went. In the loo, I carefully poured some of the juice into the specimen jar and diluted it a bit, so that it was roughly the right colour. Then I sauntered into the main clinic, leaving the glass with the rest of the juice in the kitchen.

The drugs worker looked at the specimen a bit suspiciously, holding it up to the light. I thought he was going to comment on the colour, or perhaps the strange cloudiness. Instead, he said, 'This is very cold, considering.'

Why hadn't I used warm water to dilute? 'I'm very cold-blooded,' I replied. 'Always been a problem, and now, of course, with spending so much time standing in the cold ...'

The worker looked very sceptical. 'Cold-blooded?' he said, glancing around to see if anyone was free to help him. Everyone was fully occupied.

'Yep,' I said firmly. 'It's a medical condition, so don't discriminate against me.'

He looked even more sceptical but sighed and measured out the 35ml dosage of methadone for me. I took it and left quickly, before he changed his mind. Not surprisingly, I didn't return.

The lift I had felt when I started to sell the Big Issue soon disappeared. I was trapped in a world where the drugs ruled. I was a slave, controlled and directed by the chemicals I shot into my arm. I had become so accustomed to them that they no longer gave me a high; they only prevented the nauseating, terrifying withdrawal symptoms for another day. I could not get away from my pain and loneliness any more. All that heroin did for me now was stop me from feeling extremely ill – and even that was not for long. I seemed to need more stuff more often just to maintain immunity from withdrawal.

All the feelings that I had been trying, quite successfully, to ignore for years, came flooding back. I would go back to my slovenly mess of a bedsit and just cry for hours. Even watching television didn't help in the way it once had. My emotions completely swamped me; a rising tide of grief and desperation which threatened to drown me. Without wanting to, I kept thinking of my family. I hadn't been in contact with them for two years at least, and wondered if I would ever see them again. Did they think about me, or try to find me? Or were they glad to be rid of the shame and pain that I had caused?

For the first time, I began to take a hard look at my life and where it was heading. When Jess left, I had experienced a painful self-revelation, but, not wanting to face it, had taken refuge in drugs and alcohol. Now, these were no longer providing the retreat from reality I desired. There was no escape from the inner turmoil that plagued me. I realised that despite grasping at everything I believed would solve my problems – wealth, possessions, relationships, sex, alcohol, drugs – nothing had worked. I thought that I'd found love for a while, but that thinking proved futile. I'd even tried praying a few times when I was desperate, but didn't find an answer. I didn't even know who I was praying to.

I felt as if I was standing at the edge of a huge chasm, with the ground beneath me crumbling away. At any moment, I would begin to slide down into the depths, and no one could save me. I couldn't see any point to life at all. What did my future hold? Or anybody's for that matter? Birth, school, work, marriage, work, retirement, death – was that all life was about? That seemed to be all that people aimed for – making money to buy things that didn't satisfy, and in the end to die. Only people never thought about it in that way. They just moved blindly from one stage to the next, doing what society dictated, believing all the lies and ignoring all the ways in which society failed. I was too disconnected and weary and disillusioned to be part of it.

In the midst of all this agonising depression, I continued to sell the Big Issue and to score drugs with the proceeds. I had to, otherwise the withdrawal symptoms were totally unbearable. One day, as I was standing in my usual place, I spotted Lisa coming towards me.

I had seen her quite a bit since we split up. I had been back to the house a few times, on the pretext that Ziggy was missing her, and we had remained friends. I think she was shocked that I was on the streets, and the first time she saw me there was a bit embarrassing. But she stayed to talk for a short while, and after that, used to drop by every now and then for a chat and to give me cigarettes. She very rarely gave me money, knowing how I would spend it.

Once, her sister's boyfriend, who was visiting Leeds, stopped, obviously directed to me by Lisa. Again, he didn't give me any money, but instead proffered some cans of beer. I thanked him, but when he had gone, I went inside the supermarket and sold them back. I'd never liked that brand of beer anyway.

Sometimes I wondered whether, out of the kindness of her heart, Lisa would offer to take me back, and whether I would go if she did. But she was too wise to do that, realising very clearly that I would behave exactly as before, only in a more extreme manner, since the drugs had taken an even tighter grip.

Now, when I saw her, I smiled and waved, thinking that she would probably have some cigarettes or maybe even money for me. But there was no answering smile. Lisa's face was pale and drawn. She looked as if she had been crying.

'Hi, Lisa. What's up? You look awful.' I was never one for subtleties. Ziggy danced around her, remembering that she often gave him a biscuit.

Lisa's mouth quivered as she struggled to speak. 'Oh, Ian,' she faltered, 'I don't know how to tell you ...'

'Tell me what?' I demanded, my voice rough with alarm.

'It's Tony. He's ... he's dead.'

She had started crying properly now, her shoulders shaking and tears streaming down her white face.

I staggered back as if she had hit me in the stomach. Tony – friend and partner in crime, full of life and fun. How could he be dead?

'There must be some mistake!' I shouted. 'He can't be **dead**.' But one look at her face convinced me of the truth.

She shook her head. 'I heard from my Mum. He was in a car accident on the island. They took him to hospital, but there was no hope.'

My head was whirling and I thought I was going to be sick. 'When did ... ? I must go ... the funeral ...'

Lisa interrupted as I tailed off. 'The funeral's already happened, Ian. He died ten days ago.'

I slumped down onto the supermarket steps, put my head in my hands and wept. I had known Tony since we were ten years old. We had played, got into mischief and trouble together and had always looked after each other. We shared our first spliff, we shared houses and flats, we had even shared a prison cell. We would have done anything for each other, and though I hadn't seen him for a couple of years, the bonds of friendship and a common past were still strong. I had always thought that when I finally sorted myself out, I would go back to the Isle of Man and look him up, renew the friendship. Now that could never happen.

I continued to cry, loud, ragged sobs, right there in the middle of a busy shopping street. Lisa didn't know what to do. Eventually, she went to a nearby coffee shop, and bought me a coffee. I drank it gratefully, feeling its warmth spreading to the deadly cold inside me. The reality of death confronted me with cruel clarity. I had known others who had died through drug overdoses or suicide, but somehow, their deaths, though sad, had left no impression on me. This was different. This was the brother I had left behind, the close friend who had stuck by me when no one else had. This was the person I had lost touch with, who even as he died might have wished I was there. I would never see him again, never speak to him or laugh with him. He was dead, and I felt that I couldn't bear it.

Tony had been quite a positive influence on me most of the time. He was from a stable background and seemed to do quite well at school. Subconsciously, I desired that stability, while he, on the other hand, was attracted to the adventure and excitement I appeared to be involved in. We complemented each other well and we became real soul mates. I can remember many all-night parties, where we would just sit around and talk about every issue under the sun.

Often our most passionate discussions centred on getting pot legalised. I remember clearly our first experiments with the drug. These comprised various trials with banana skins. We'd heard, as I'm sure countless others had at the time, that you could get high smoking the skins if you prepared them in a certain way. Well, we boiled them, grilled them, sun-baked them, scraped the inner white bit off. You certainly couldn't accuse us of not giving it a proper go! But in the end we had to admit defeat. The only sensation we got from smoking them was a headache! The banana skins were meant to be the next progression from glue sniffing. Then some older boys, who must have heard of our exploits, offered to take us for a smoke of pot. We agreed readily and went off to their smoking den – a Jaguar parked up in a garage. It was a very covert, and therefore highly exciting, operation, as smoking pot on the Isle of Man was an imprisonable offence. We shared one joint between us and Tony and I were both very sick when we hit the fresh air outside the garage, to the jeers of the older boys. I think they just wanted to laugh at us in our inexperience, which, naturally, made us determined to become hardened pot-smokers. We left it for a month or so, though.

In the meantime, Tony and I experimented with magic mushrooms. Again, it seemed we were destined for failure and certain illness. We kept picking the wrong ones. By this time, there were a few other lads involved. I remember one night in particular there were about seven of us and we managed to pick a few hundred of what we thought was the right variety. We shared them all out, squabbling down to the last one. After eating the disgusting-tasting things and managing not to be sick, we waited. An hour later, we were still waiting for something to happen, thinking that they should surely be working by now. We decided to go to the steepest hill in the town and sprint up it, as we thought that this would get the drug pumping around our bodies more quickly. After three attempts at this, we gave up. Even we, in our naivety, realised that the effect wasn't meant to be a heart attack!

Our next attempt proved to be more 'successful', as it nearly ended up with a visit to the local psychiatric hospital. One boy was having serious hallucinations, thinking that the stones and buildings were all people out to get him. Tony and I managed to calm him down, while at the same time trying to cope with our own demons. It got to about two o'clock in the morning and they both went home, leaving me alone. I was still very much under the influence of the hallucinogen and was scared, so there was no way I was going home. Instead, I sat on the back step of our house for another two hours, trying not to give way to panic. I thought I was never going to come out of this mad hallucinating state. At about five in the morning, I finally recovered sufficiently to go in and go to bed, but was afraid to open my eyes the following morning in case it all started again. Thankfully, I discovered that I was back to normal and said to myself,

'Never again!' This, however, proved to be a hollow promise; one I would often hear myself and others saying in the years to come.

I was often blamed for leading my mates astray, but we usually egged one another on, especially Tony and I. Tony was a bit of a fighter, though he never went looking for trouble. He was very thin and didn't have much meat on him, but he was very quick and wouldn't think twice of tackling somebody much bigger than himself. Sometimes, in our drugged state, we would argue with each other and even end up fighting. Funnily enough though, this seemed to strengthen our friendship. He taught me a lot about courage and about sticking by each other. There were many, many times when he was the only friend I had. And now he was gone.

I didn't know what to do or say. I wanted to go away and shut out the world. But as I sat there, familiar sensations of nausea and shaking began to surge through me. The severe shock I had received and the accompanying strong emotions had caused an early onset of withdrawal symptoms. Though I wanted to walk away, I couldn't. I had to stay and make enough money to get some drugs. Tony's death suddenly put my whole life into a different perspective. I was filled with a self-disgust so bitter that I was nearly sick.

While I stood there, trying to sell the Big Issue, with my head full of memories of Tony and images of what his last moments might have been like, a man shuffled right up to me. He was a familiar sight around the area, muttering and occasionally shouting to passers-by. This time it was me he had a problem with, and he started yelling obscenities about the Big Issue and my selling of it. Normally, I would have tolerated him for a bit before sending him on his way, but this time I was seized with a huge, unmanageable anger. At that moment, I wanted to kill him, to pour onto this irritating but essentially harmless man all the impotent rage I felt at Tony's death and my life. Controlling myself with an effort, I shouted out to him to go away, that I had just heard that my best friend was dead and that I wasn't in the mood for hassle. He looked at my face and he believed me. With a sheepish grin and a muttered apology, he sloped off up the road. I stuffed the rest of the magazines into my bag and headed for home, still shaking with anger and grief.

Over the next few days, I came to realise the evil depths that heroin and its like had brought me to. The black cloud of depression that had been hovering over me for a long time completely enveloped me now. Even some of my customers, who rarely spent more than a minute or so with me, noticed a difference. A couple of them asked what was wrong and I told them the sad story. Two kind people, who had been customers for quite some time, returned with substantial gifts of money to enable me to go back to the Isle of Man to see Tony's family. I accepted the money with a show of gratitude, but instead of getting on a train, I wasted the lot on crack and heroin and got completely stoned. It was still the only way I knew to deal with the amount of pain I was experiencing. Even though I understood that the drugs were destroying me, I couldn't stop.

A few days later, one of the ladies who had given me the money asked how I had got on. I told her that her money had been stolen by another street trader. She was shocked, and promptly gave me the same amount again. I hated myself for doing it, but I took the money and yet again squandered it on crack and heroin. The need for drugs outweighed any faint pangs of conscience I may have felt. Part of me longed to go back to the Isle of Man and share my grief with Tony's family and receive some comfort. But I was also bitterly upset that I had missed the funeral, and couldn't see the point of going back now, when all the public mourning was over and everyone was trying to get back to normal. Thanks to the misplaced kindness of my customer, I was able to take a trip of a different kind, not back to my friend's last resting place, but into my familiar world of unreality and escape.

I didn't stay in that world for long though. All too soon, from my point of view, I returned to consciousness and the bleak blackness of my situation. I lay on my bed in my squalid bedsit and wept. I felt totally without hope and without help. I cried for Tony and for Jess, for my lost childhood and my empty future. I cried for my Gran and my Dad and for the mother I never had.

Gradually, as I grew calmer, my mind drifted over the past and all of a sudden, I felt as if I was lying on the beach again, like I used to as a child. I wondered for a moment whether I was having another drug rush, but knew I was sober. I remembered my excitement when I used to dash in and out of the waves, and the sense of achievement when I built a sandcastle. Then another image flashed into my mind; a man standing on the beach with an easel, telling a story and drawing at the same time. A crowd of children watching and listening with rapt attention. The snake and the woman and the apple. What was that all about?

The story came back to me as clearly as if the man was in my bedsit telling it, and I remembered how God had been forced to send Adam and Eve out of the perfect garden because they had chosen to disobey him. I remembered the sadness I had felt at such an unhappy ending. I could see the man standing there, smiling at his small audience and saying, 'But God **did** make it a happy ending – many, many years later. He loved everyone in the world he had made, and he didn't want them to suffer. He wanted them to be his friends again. So, he sent his son Jesus to make it right.'

Slow tears oozed down my cheeks as I remembered the man's words of explanation, showing that Jesus, totally perfect in every way, took on the punishment for **all** the wrong and evil things ever done from Adam onwards. He spoke a lot about God's love, and how Jesus' death made that love available to everyone again. Somehow, in the memory and the words there was a flicker of hope, a beckoning towards the cleanness and innocence of that childhood day. I didn't understand, and continued to weep, but this time, there was healing in my tears.

Just as I was beginning to feel that there were no tears left, from deep inside me, a huge cry erupted. All the pain and the disillusionment, all the rejection and hatred in my whole life were contained in that desperate, primeval howl.

'God help me!' I shouted into the silence.

CHAPTER SEVEN
A new life

'So, do you want to come along, then?'

'Sorry, mate? I wasn't quite with you,' I apologised, focusing on my customer. He was a regular, and often stopped for a bit of a chat. Normally, I only listened to my customers with half an ear, hoping that by nodding and smiling occasionally, I would get a bit more money from them. This time, though, the man had mentioned Jesus. This in itself was a bit odd – not many people spoke about him, unless swearing – and this bloke sounded like he knew him. This had made me think, particularly after my strange experience a few days before. Nothing had happened after I had shouted out to God. There were no flashing lights or voices from heaven. Just silence, but with it a curiously peaceful feeling that things were going to get better.

'I was asking you if you wanted to come along for a meal,' said the man, smiling. 'It's at a local church – food and then a chat about Christianity.'

I was usually up for a free meal, even if it meant putting up with a 'chat' afterwards. Still, I wasn't sure. 'Well, it sounds good, but I've got the dog, see. He goes everywhere with me.'

'That's OK,' said my customer readily, 'he can come too.'

I was surprised, and no longer had an excuse to refuse, so I agreed to go.

A few days later, then, saw Ziggy and me going for a rare evening out. I had even smoothed my hair – and his – in honour of the occasion! I found the church fairly easily and climbed up the steps to the door. I couldn't believe that I was really just about to go into a church. I had always disliked church buildings, right from childhood. To me, they represented boring religion; the 'fancy hat brigade' going through the motions of ritual once a week to make out they were better than the rest of us. In recent years, the only contact I'd had with churches was to break in and steal from them.

My customer, who, I discovered, was called Steve, was waiting in the doorway, and seemed very pleased to see me. I immediately felt out of place. It seemed an extremely long time since I had been in a decent environment, amongst ordinary people. There were about 15 other people in the main hall and no other dogs. Ziggy, though, seemed perfectly at home, and I envied him his social ease.

The meal was delicious, the best I'd eaten for years. I didn't say a lot, although people kept trying to include me in the conversation. Everyone seemed lively and happy and the meal was quite a laugh. I was surprised. I expected church people to be serious and strict, but these were joking about all sorts of things, and teasing one another all the time. I began to relax a little.

In fact, I relaxed a little too much. After the meal, we all sat down in a circle to have a discussion. I don't know whether it was the effects of a much needed meal, the atmosphere or – more likely – the heroin I had scored before coming, but I became extremely sleepy. Within a few minutes of the beginning of the discussion, I had fallen fast asleep. When someone shook me awake gently at the end, I was highly embarrassed. With muttered thanks for the meal, I left quickly, a reluctant Ziggy at my heels. He had liked it there too, and had also been fed.

It made a good story among the other Big Issue traders, and we had a laugh about how interesting the discussion must have been. One of the vendors, Nicky, seemed quite keen on the idea of a free meal. 'Cor, I wish it had been me he'd asked,' he said. 'I could do with a meal like that. I bet I wouldn't have fallen asleep. You've wrecked your chances there, mate. Send him my way next time!'

I knew there wouldn't be a next time. I had indeed wrecked my chances of another lovely meal, and besides, I would be too embarrassed to see all those people again. I was astonished, therefore, later that same day, to see Steve coming towards me, still smiling.

'Hi there Ian!' He greeted me as if we were old buddies. I grunted and looked at the pavement. Steve made a fuss of Ziggy and then said, 'It was nice to have you round last night. Would you like to come again next week?'

I didn't know what to say. I couldn't believe that he would want me to come again, when I had rudely gone to sleep in the middle of the talking. Then I remembered Nicky. 'Well, er, that's nice of you. I was telling my mate about it, and he seemed quite interested. Could he come along as well, like?'

Nothing seemed to faze Steve. 'Of course he can,' he said heartily. 'We'll expect you. Same time, same place!' He bought a Big Issue and strode off. I stared after him in disbelief. Had I really agreed to go back there? I couldn't wait to tell Nicky!

The following week, Nicky, Ziggy and I made our way to the church. Both Nicky and I had injected with heroin before leaving. It was our prop to help us get through a potentially difficult situation. Neither of us was capable of facing anything new or challenging in our own strength. Only sustained with heroin did we feel able to approach the church building and the people inside.

Once more we were made welcome, and the meal was tasty and filling. Nicky was fairly ill-at-ease, but tucked into his food with gusto. I felt more familiar with the whole situation and was able to join in a little more with the conversation. When it came to the after-dinner discussion, however, an awful sense of déjà vu prevailed, only this time, it wasn't just me who couldn't keep his eyes open. Nicky had dropped off almost immediately, and I was not far behind. Even Ziggy settled down for a quick snooze.

'Ian! Ian! Wake up man. You've gone to sleep again!' I sat up with a jerk, completely disorientated.

Steve had his face right up against mine and was shaking me. He seemed a bit agitated. 'Come on now, try and stay awake. It's a bit rude to ignore everyone else like this.'

I was indignant. He shouldn't show me up like this in public. 'I **wasn't** asleep. I was just resting my eyes. 'Course I was listening,' I said, not very convincingly.

Steve sat back down, politely accepting my explanation. I kicked Nicky awake, and after a short while, we made our escape. I didn't say much to Steve or the others as I left, because I felt so completely ashamed.

Nicky chuckled all the way back. 'Did I say I wouldn't fall asleep?' he asked. 'That place must cast some sort of spell. You know, like *Sleeping Beauty*!' He laughed raucously at his feeble joke. 'Good meal though. Worth it for that!'

I didn't say anything, suspecting that somehow, I had lost more than I had gained.

True to form, Steve turned up again the next day and, unbelievably, invited us back for a meal the following week. I made up an excuse this time, feeling that I couldn't face everyone again after two weeks of embarrassment. There was always the risk that I would fall asleep for a third time. I had to admire the man. He didn't give up. Every week he would come, buy a Big Issue and invite me to something or other. At first it was a continuation of the discussion group, then there were barbecues, talks, a talent evening. It seemed as if there was always something going on at this church of his. I always had an excuse for not accepting his invitations, although actually all I did instead was sit in my miserable dump of a bedsit watching junk television. Occasionally, someone else from the original meal would also stop at my pitch for a chat and to make a fuss of Ziggy. They would always invite me to an event as well.

I resisted all these attempts to enliven my social life, for nearly six months. During this time, the drugs tightened their grip on me. My health deteriorated and I looked and felt like an old man. I needed more and more frequent fixes in order to stay at the same level. The minute anything went wrong, or I was feeling upset, I had to inject straight away to cope. I woke up every morning shaking and nauseous, my whole body screaming for a fix.

One morning, after the first few feverish minutes of struggle and horror had changed to unnatural calm, I found that my mind was very clear. I looked hard at my present situation, and wondered what my life would be like in ten years' time. I might still be on the streets, living in this pit, only in a far worse physical and mental state than this. I might be in prison or I might well be dead, killed by the drugs that had caused a living death for so many years.

I thought about the two meals I had enjoyed at the church. It wasn't just the food that had made it a special time. I had liked the kindness and acceptance of the people, the laughter and fun, the normal conversation. When they talked about Jesus, it was natural. Their faith wasn't something extra to be worn like a badge for all to see; it was part of them, like their clothes. I hadn't heard a word of what was said in the discussions on those two evenings, yet those people accepted me as

I was – a stinking, dishevelled tramp-like figure – and that spoke more than a thousand words could ever do.

I realised that as well as feeling embarrassed, I had held back from the church thing out of a sort of pride. What would my friends and family say if they knew I was getting involved in religion? I would be so teased by the other Big Issue sellers and beggars. Ironically, we all thought people who went to church were a bit weird. I suppose that normality is in the eye of the beholder, in the same way as beauty.

As I lay there that morning, my thoughts illuminated with unusual clarity, I came to the decision that I didn't want to stay this way any more. The opinions of my friends and family were not very relevant, for the hard truth was that I no longer had friends or family. I had nothing except my dog and a destructive need for drugs. I didn't want my life to end in waste and degradation. A future that continued in this hell of loneliness, self-disgust and enslavement was intolerable. Anything had to be better than that. I decided that if Steve invited me to anything else, I would accept.

I didn't see him for a few days after that and I had a sudden fear that after all this time he **had** given up.

Then one day, I saw him striding along as usual as if he didn't have a care in the world. He spotted me and smiled a greeting. I smiled back, for once genuinely pleased to see someone and not just cynically pretending in order to make a sale.

'Hey, Ian! Do you fancy coming to a do at church on Friday?'

'What's going off?' I asked, not wanting to seem too keen.

'Well, there's a good band playing, then this American guy is giving a bit of a talk.'

My first thought was 'Hmm, some dodgy American. He'll just be after my money.' Then, I realised that I was quite safe because I didn't have any money! I decided that I would go, and that I would **not** fall asleep.

Steve arranged to meet me at the door of the church. For once, I'd left Ziggy behind in the bedsit, and I felt a bit insecure without him. He was undoubtedly a sort of prop for me. When I walked in, I was amazed at how different the building seemed from when I'd come for the meals all those months ago. There were so many people milling about, and the buzz was amazing. The room was set out very informally, with large round tables dotted about, all attractively decorated. I didn't expect church to be so noisy – it was almost like walking into a pub or club (without the cigarettes and alcohol, of course!). A band was warming up on the stage, playing through seriously big speakers, and it sounded good. Attractive girls were shrieking with delight as they greeted one another and even older people were giving each other warm hugs. There was a great atmosphere of excitement.

Steve and I sat down at a table, though he kept getting up to chat to people. He seemed to know practically everybody, and introduced me to quite a few, but mostly I kept my head down. Then the band started properly, and I forgot my self-consciousness in the sheer pleasure of it all. It was so long since I had sat and listened to live music, and the band was surprisingly good. The audience was very enthusiastic, dancing in the spaces between tables and at the front, and joining in some of the singing. I began to relax and enjoy myself.

There was a good variety of music, some really loud and lively, some quiet and thoughtful. I could have gone on listening, but after a while, someone came onto the stage to announce the next item. The band was cheered off and people went back to their seats, some of them quite red-faced with exertion.

It was time for the dodgy American. He was much younger than I expected; a stocky, good-looking young man, casually dressed, with the clean-cut, strong jaw and perfect smile of the stereotypical American. The stereotypes ended there though. This man, also a Steven, was a brilliant speaker – funny, passionate, interesting, dramatic and down-to-earth. Most of the time, I felt as if he was speaking just to me.

Gradually, as I listened, all the different pieces of my jigsaw fell into place. I had looked for a depth and excitement in drugs and drink that the world hadn't given me. From an early age, I had seen life as pretty shallow; chasing after money, going clubbing at weekends, then by the time you reached thirty-something it was over, time to settle down with your mortgage, wife and 2.2 kids. I couldn't deny some of those things were good but surely there was more? What was the meaning of it all?

As I continued to listen eagerly to the speaker, I remembered again the story I had heard as a child, of Adam and Eve, who had everything perfect and then blew it by disobeying God and going their own way. Suddenly, I understood how Jesus did 'make it right' after all, for Adam and Eve and for all of us who came after them. I heard the story of his agonising death and his resurrection and felt like crying as I realised he had gone through all that so that I could be forgiven. I considered again the misery of my present life and all the things I had done wrong in it. I had a sudden certainty of the existence of God, and of his overwhelming love and forgiveness for me. He had been holding out His hand to me for years but I had to make the choice. It was incredible. Nothing I had ever heard before made as much sense as this.

Then the speaker drew his talk to a close by asking everyone to pray. Slightly embarrassed, I bowed my head and listened to his prayer, my heart beating fast:

'Lord Jesus, thank you that you died for me, so that I could be forgiven and set free. I am sorry for the things that I have done wrong in my life. Please forgive me and help me to turn from everything that I know is wrong. Thank you for that forgiveness and your Holy Spirit. Please come into my life and be with me forever. Amen.'

'Amen,' muttered hundreds of people. I was about to look up, when Steven started speaking again.

'Now, I believe that there are some people here who have prayed that prayer for the first time this evening. If that is you, and you really meant it, please raise your hand while everyone's eyes are closed, so that I can pray for you.'

I felt paralysed. I wanted so much to acknowledge that I **had** prayed that prayer, that I accepted all that had been said. But I was terrified of someone seeing me. I hated the thought of all the attention I would receive. I sat on the edge of my seat, every passing second stretching the agony of indecision. All around me, people had their eyes closed. Only the speaker was looking – straight at me or so it seemed. Suddenly, I was hit by the thought that if I didn't do this now, tonight, I might never get another chance. It was enough to decide me, and slowly, shakily, I raised my hand a fraction. Steven smiled and nodded, and my hand shot down again. It felt as if it was the most courageous thing I had ever done.

There were still no flashing lights or peals of thunder, but this time I felt very sure that something significant and life changing had happened. I knew that I had meant what I had prayed from the bottom of my heart, and felt a strange sense of peace about it. Steven prayed again and then finished by asking those who had become Christians to tell someone what had happened. I turned to the person on the other side of me – it was easier in a way to say this to a stranger – and said, 'I've just become a Christian!' It sounded odd in my ears, but wonderful as well. Hearing myself say it made it all the more real.

My neighbour seemed delighted with the news, and gave me a huge hug, before yelling to Steve, who was sitting on the other side of me, 'Great news, Steve! He's become a Christian!'

Steve's whoop of joy could have been heard in Bradford. He also gave me a huge hug, as well as slapping me heartily on the back. I began to feel like a celebrity.

I was introduced to Steve's friend Stuart, and they asked if they could pray with me before I went home, to 'be filled with the Holy Spirit'. I gave them a quizzical look. This was something new to me, and I wasn't sure what it entailed. However, I agreed to go with them into a side room that was a bit quieter.

'We'll pray for a bit, and ask God's Holy Spirit to fill you. Don't worry if we start laughing – sometimes that's how it affects us.'

I was even more puzzled now, and a bit uneasy. They began praying, and sure enough, after a short while, they both started laughing, not manically, but just as if something was making them very happy. I didn't like this at all. It felt as if they were laughing at me. I was just about to say something when they both went quiet. For quite a while, we just sat there, with nothing much appearing to happen. Finally, I broke the silence.

'Listen, guys, it's nice of you to pray for me, but if this Holy Spirit doesn't show up in the next five minutes, I'm off home.' They nodded understandingly and began to pray for me again, resting their hands lightly on my shoulders.

Within a few minutes, something very odd happened. I could feel an intense heat in the pit of my stomach, which then spread to the rest of my body. I had never before experienced anything quite like it. The sensation was undeniable; powerful, but not painful. With it came the most intense feeling of peace. I felt as if I was in a huge state of shock, but it was not unpleasant – quite the reverse in fact. I opened my mouth to comment on what was happening, and what came out was a different language. It was my voice, but it wasn't English. Instead of being amazed or frightened, I just felt elated. I carried on speaking, not knowing exactly what I was saying, but knowing that it was to do with God and Jesus, and that it was good.

I carried on speaking in this strange language for about ten minutes – the longest I had ever spoken without a pause! All this time, I had a feeling of excitement and pure joy inside. It was the most incredible experience, and not one that I could have possibly manufactured.

Finally, I came to a stop, my jaw aching somewhat, and looked at Steve and Stuart in a bit of a daze. They were grinning away like Cheshire cats.

'What happened there?' I asked a bit shakily. 'It was amazing.'

'You've been filled with the Holy Spirit of God,' said Stuart. 'It's God's way of being with you and giving you the power you need to live his way.'

I didn't really understand what he meant at that point, but I knew that what had happened was real.

I went home feeling completely different. I was still a bit dazed, but beneath that rather floating feeling, there was a new core of complete peace and joy. When I got back to the bedsit, Ziggy was absolutely ecstatic to see me. I told him all about the evening, and then, out of habit, reached for my syringe, which was ready for use. I hesitated, but the routine was so well instilled, and the fear of withdrawal so strong, that I injected the drug without another thought.

The following morning, I felt dreadful. My first day as a Christian, and I had let God down totally by using drugs – something I knew he didn't want. I was still completely sure that what had happened the previous evening was real, and I wanted a fresh start. But achieving that was obviously going to be harder than I thought. The guilt I felt was almost as bad as the withdrawal symptoms. I had to keep using, because I couldn't cope physically or mentally without a fix, but I knew that I was doing wrong.

Steve came to see me during the day, and I told him about the problems I was having. He was very sympathetic, and made me realise that God always gives us another chance if we ask him. He had read a book by the missionary Jackie Pullinger, who had worked among heroin addicts in Hong Kong. Her strategy was to put each addict alongside someone who would encourage them, look after them and pray over them when they got into a severe state of withdrawal. Many, many addicts who had become Christians had come off drugs in a miraculously short space of time. Steve suggested that whenever I felt the need for a fix, I should 'pray in tongues'. Apparently, this is what I had been doing the night before when I spoke in a different language. Steve explained that it is a way of praying that bypasses the mind and communicates directly with God's Spirit. I was fascinated at the thought that I could choose to do this, though, as Steve pointed out, it would only happen when I was wanting to pray or worship. It was not a formula or a mantra.

Altogether, I was amazed at what I was learning about my new life as a Christian. I found that I could talk to God, and I learnt an important lesson at that time; one that I still endeavour to apply to this day, and that is always to be real with God. I termed it being 'real-igious not re-ligious'. I discovered that I could be myself with God without being in any way disrespectful. It was an extraordinary blend of relating to him as an awesome

King and also as my Dad, with whom I could chat about anything. Even stranger was the fact that it was not difficult to communicate on two such different levels at the same time.

I also continued to be able to pray 'in tongues', weird though that seemed. Whenever I did, I felt an amazing power surge through me. At first, I found that I was repeating the same phrase again and again. Whenever I began to pray in this spiritual language, these were the only words that came out. This puzzled and frustrated me, so I decided to ask someone about it.

'Why don't you ask God what the words mean?' was his suggestion. I thought this was a good idea, so, the next time I was praying, I asked God what the words meant, and why they were all I seemed to say.

Instantly, the words seemed to go into slow motion, and I could decipher them. Then, the words 'I am like a lamb' kept sounding in my mind. All these weeks, I had been praying, 'I am like a lamb'! I was not impressed. In fact, I felt a bit affronted. I didn't consider myself to be lamb-like, so why would I be saying that to God? After my initial feelings of offence had subsided, it dawned on me that it was all to do with pride. By admitting to God that

I was a lamb – vulnerable, not very bright, needing help, following the Shepherd – I was getting rid of my pride and becoming humble. It must have taken a long time because even in my spirit, I was quite stubborn! I felt very excited as I realised the truth of what I was thinking, and started to pray again, thanking God for all that he was doing. Immediately, a torrent of beautiful new words came pouring out of my mouth as I thought about how good God is. My new language of prayer and praise expanded from that day.

I began to look at the Bible, since everyone said that it was important to read it. I found it quite difficult to understand much at first, but I kept going with it. All those hours spent reading when I was in prison were paying off at last. Sometimes, I would read something in the Bible that seemed to be aimed directly at me, answering an unspoken question or hidden need. That was exciting, but for much of the time, I struggled to make sense of it all.

The first time I went along to a Sunday service, I wondered what on earth had hit me. My previous experience of church services was very limited, and my memories were of boredom and resentment.

This, however, was very different. Though externally conventional, the building was light and colourful inside, with lots of space. There was not the hushed silence and quiet sitting of my memory, but lots of noise and movement as everyone greeted one another and caught up on news. When we actually began the service, a band struck up a very lively number and everyone joined in energetically. Some people danced, others waved their arms in the air, still more stood singing heartily with one or both hands raised. The song was projected onto a screen, and when we had sung it, I was surprised to find that we then started it again – and again. No one seemed to tire of singing, and the words obviously meant a lot to them. When eventually there was a lull, I was amazed to hear all sorts of people pray from the congregation, as well as the leader. This was not church as I knew it!

The very exuberance that in some ways was so attractive, was in other ways a bit intimidating. I felt embarrassed at times because I didn't know what was happening, and because, frankly, it all seemed a bit weird. When everyone began singing all together in strange languages, I felt the hairs rise on the back of my neck. What had I got into? Yet, despite this natural reaction, I still felt that inner peace which had been with me since becoming a Christian. The atmosphere in the church was not threatening or spooky; it was full of love and joy. Meeting people afterwards, I could see their genuine love, and their love for what Jesus had done in their lives, and this showed in their worship.

I was also, slowly but surely, making new friends. Years of rejection and loneliness had left me extremely lacking in confidence and I didn't expect anyone to take much notice of me. After all, I was an addict, a 'rough and ready' street person, living in squalor. But, to my surprise, everyone accepted me and made quite a fuss of me. I was invited round to people's houses for meals, and included in anything that was happening in the church. Several of the young men, particularly Steve and Stuart, spent lots of time with me helping me to learn more about God, and praying with me. Other people gave me practical help. This continuing acceptance and care was amazing. I had lived for so long in a tough world where I had to be totally self-sufficient to survive, that I found it hard to cope with real love and openness when it was offered to me.

This group of people had such a different 'take' on life from my own. Their values and lifestyle were radically opposite to anything I had ever known – and as far as I could see, they were genuine. Even at this early stage in my Christian life, I realised that they were motivated and empowered by something beyond themselves. I wanted what they had, and believed that they would be able to help me learn more of the Jesus I had so recently come to know.

Since that evening when I had shakily put my hand up and made the decision to follow Jesus, life had not suddenly become easy and straightforward. There was no fairy godmother waving a wand to make it all OK. I knew I had many challenges to face if I wanted my life to turn round. And I did. I had lived my past opposed to God, glimpsed a future without him and had wonderfully experienced an instant of the present with him. I knew which direction I had chosen to go – there was no contest. The strangeness of this new way of life was difficult to adapt to, but I didn't want to let go of it. At last, I had hope.

CHAPTER EIGHT
The drugs fight back

Ziggy growled and bared his teeth at the person approaching us. It was a poorly dressed man, pale-faced and loitering rather than walking purposefully along the street. He didn't look at all threatening, so I wasn't sure why the dog was objecting. As the man drew nearer, I recognised him as a dealer in the Chapeltown area. I hadn't had a lot to do with him, but knew he had a reputation as a hard man. He was smiling now though, as he stopped to speak to me.

'Heard you're thinking of giving up on the heroin,' he said.

I nodded. 'Yeah, I've had enough. I'm on a methadone programme.'

The man's face showed disgust. 'Those c*** things. Can't stand them. Still, you could get some extra methadone, I suppose?'

'Shouldn't think so,' I replied, 'they're very strict these days. Besides, I want to go clean this time.'

He leaned a bit closer to me, confidentially. The smell of stale tobacco and body odour made me want to step back, but I stayed put. Ziggy growled again, menacingly.

'Look, I wouldn't do this for everyone, but you're a regular round here, aren't you. I can let you have a bag of stuff for nothing. Straight on.'

I could hardly believe my ears. I had lived in Chapeltown for years and had never been offered free heroin. It was unheard of! It was surely no coincidence that this was my first week off heroin. Someone or something was trying to get me back.

I thanked the man but refused and walked away as quickly as possible and continued towards my Big Issue pitch. I had only been walking for about quarter of an hour when someone else came up to me. To my astonishment, it was another dealer.

'I heard you hadn't got any stuff at the moment,' he said, hiding his face from passers-by.

'No. I'm coming off it. Methadone,' I said tersely, not wanting to be seen with this notorious dealer.

'Well, I've got a bag here you can have for free,' he said, as if he was doing me a favour.

'Thanks, but no thanks. Must go, I'm late.' With that I hurried off, wondering how many other people were going to offer me freebies that morning.

This was just one more obstacle of the many that seemed to confront me as I struggled to come off drugs. I had taken Steve's advice and prayed in tongues when the withdrawal symptoms began, but this had only had limited success. When I was with Christian friends, and when I was in the church services, there was nothing I wanted more than to get rid of the habit and be obedient to God. But somehow, when I was in the familiar environment of my pitch or the bedsit, the routine and demands of my pre-Christian life seemed to take over. My body and mind craved the excitement of a drug-rush, as well as needing it chemically. Drug-taking was my existence. I had known nothing else for over 15 years. It was hard to begin a new lifestyle from scratch.

Steve managed to get me an appointment with his GP, and she was sympathetic. I think she could see that I was sincere in wanting to come off drugs. Once more, I was put on a methadone programme, based at the surgery, rather than the clinic, and this time it was working. She calculated that I would need a certain amount of time to be weaned off methadone, but I was determined to do it in less, sure that with God's help, it was possible. I stopped taking heroin, and felt so much better in myself. Although methadone is a heroin substitute, and therefore just as addictive, being on the programme meant that I was being monitored and could gradually lessen the dose. It seemed like medication for an illness rather than an illicit hobby. It was clean, safe and legal. I felt that I had taken the first steps in obeying God.

Now, though, I was being tempted in the most extraordinary way to go back on my decision. Never before had I been offered free stuff, and suddenly dealers were appearing from nowhere to give it away. I had resisted this time, but I had been tempted. I missed the thrill of the effects of the drug – that rush just after shooting up had become as vital as food and drink to me.

A new, subtler temptation presented itself to me, and this time, I didn't resist. Because I had stopped taking heroin, and the methadone was free, I had a bit of money to spare. This would have been a good opportunity to buy some new clothes, perhaps consider somewhere else to live or even give something to the church, but my mindset was still in the old ways. I began to buy crack cocaine; a drug I had experimented with a bit in the past, but had not used seriously. It was extremely addictive. I found that the effects lasted a very short time and the need for more was almost immediate. Soon, I was taking as much crack as I used to take heroin.

The battle between drugs and God raged on. I certainly knew from experience what the writer Paul meant when he wrote in a letter:

I have the desire to do what is good, but I cannot carry it out. For what I do is not the good I want to do; no, the evil I do not want to do – this I keep on doing. (Romans 7:18b–19, NIV.)

I felt as if I was two people; the new Christian who yearned to know more of God and Jesus and to follow this way which seemed so good, and the addict who could not escape the physical and mental demands of evil drugs. Though I had taken a step into a new life, I was still living in my old world and when I was there, I naturally fell into all my old ways of thinking and acting.

Even though I was secretly and guiltily continuing to take new drugs, I also had some amazing experiences of God. I could not deny the reality of my encounters with him, even though cynics might scoff and talk of coincidence. I was gradually discovering the power of prayer in many different areas. Previously, when I had come off heroin, I had suffered badly from sleep deprivation. This time, though, having found a verse in the Psalms which said that 'the Lord grants sleep to those he loves', I prayed each night as I went to bed that he would grant me sleep, and slept like a baby!

On another occasion, when the holes in my boots were really bothering me, I asked God for a new pair. That very night, when I went to a friend's house for a meal, he greeted me at the door holding a new pair of boots my size. I nearly fell off the step in shock! I knew that God didn't have to answer my prayer like that. He could have said, 'Use the money you earn on boots instead of drugs.' But he wanted to show me how very much he loved me by answering me so specifically and supernaturally. This incident had a great effect on my relationship with God. I was excited by the way it had happened, and reassured by the security of being loved unconditionally.

In many such ways, the gap between my old life and my new life became wider and more difficult to keep up. This was brought home to me very clearly one evening after I got home from a day's Big Issue selling. When I arrived at the bedsit, I found Stan, a fellow addict, waiting for me. Over the years, he had often come round to my place to shoot up. This time, however, he wanted me to sell him some drugs. I refused, and explained that I wasn't dealing and that I wanted to come off the drugs altogether. Stan, already in the throes of withdrawal, didn't take this very well. He started to swear at me, trying to persuade me to give him something.

Just as things were getting very uncomfortable, and I was wondering how to get out of the situation, I heard my doorbell ring. Peering out of the window, I saw that it was Stuart from church. What a dilemma! Inside, I had Stan, using highly obscene and abusive language, desperate for a fix. Outside, was Stuart, gentle, caring and ready for a fun night out with friends. The two parts of my life were about to come into painful conflict with each other. Stuart might be loving and good, but he was straight-talking as well. I didn't want to lose status in his sight. With great difficulty, I hustled Stan out of the back door. He was still yelling abuse as he staggered down the road. The one which hit home was 'you f****** hypocrite'.

I went round to the front door and let Stuart in. It was all too close for comfort. I decided that I couldn't go on living this double life. But I didn't say anything to Stuart. I was still too proud to let him know what a mess I was making of my faith. I was too afraid of rejection.

Later that night, as I was lying in bed, I heard a banging on the bedsit door. Then a familiar voice shouted at me to let him in. It was Stan, obviously still in a desperate state, and very angry. I decided to lay low and pretend I was out. Maybe Stan would go away. This was false optimism. When knocking failed to rouse me, he began kicking the door, yelling insults with every kick. I hid under the bedclothes, feeling quite alarmed by now and praying frantically. There was no hope that anyone else in the house would come to my aid. They were too drunk, and besides, such loud noises were too commonplace to be noticed.

Suddenly, it all went quiet. I listened to his footsteps going unsteadily down the stairs and breathed a sigh of relief, thanking God for answering my prayers. I lay still, waiting for my heart to slow down a bit, and then turned over to get some sleep. Just as I was drifting off, an almighty bang practically shot me out of the bed. Stan had returned – and this time with some sort of tool to help him. The banging increased and I could hear the sound of tearing wood. Finally, with a violent crash, the door and frame came away and Stan burst in. He grabbed a bit of the door frame, which had nails sticking out of it, and advanced towards the bed, breathing heavily. I lay under the covers, hardly daring to breathe.

'Right, you b******. You give me some stuff now or I'll do you in. You hear me? Give me some NOW!'

He started hitting the bed wildly, the nails catching on the sheets. A blow fell on me and I leapt out, grabbing a nearby broken pool cue, which was lying in a pile of other rubbish near the bed.

'That's it! I've had enough of you!' I yelled, furiously angry myself by now, as well as frightened. I started laying into him with the pool cue, beating him back across the room. We must have looked like two crazy fencing opponents.

Stan backed away from my onslaught and out of the room. I couldn't leave him there though, particularly as I no longer had a door to my bedsit. I continued chasing him down the stairs and out of the front door, yelling at him all the while and threatening him with all sorts if he should come back again. After a hundred yards or so, I stopped, watching him run off down the road, fairly sure that he would not return again. It was only then that I realised I was standing in the middle of the street, clutching a broken pool cue and wearing only boxer shorts!

The incident was a wake-up call for me. It shocked me into facing the stark contrast between the two lives I had been trying to run simultaneously. Stan was right; I **was** a hypocrite, hiding my sins from my Christian friends, not letting them see what I was really like. I decided that I could no longer bear to go on like this. For the first time in many, many years,

I had a guilty conscience and it was making me too uncomfortable. I had to do something about it. I knew that what I **wanted** to do was walk away completely from the world of drugs, but it just seemed too difficult to do. Even as I was agonising over the situation, I was still taking crack. Maybe the answer was to give up being a Christian? At least then I wouldn't be so aware of what God wanted and what I couldn't seem to achieve. Yet the thought of doing that was awful. I had found something so wonderful; I didn't want to lose it again and go back to how I had been before.

To clear my conscience, whatever happened afterwards, I knew that I would have to confess what I had been doing to someone at church. Stuart was the obvious choice, since he had been one of my first points of contact and had remained supportive and involved. It wasn't easy though. I felt physically sick when I arrived there, and spent the whole service on the edge of my seat, afraid to say anything, yet unable to do anything until I had. Eventually, when I got to the point at which I thought I would explode with the pressure, and under the cover of a time of prayer, I turned to Stuart and told him everything. I could feel my cheeks burning as I talked about the crack and the extent to which I had become addicted. I told him of his narrow escape from meeting Stan, and all that had happened that night. I admitted how difficult I was finding it to stop needing and wanting drugs.

Having talked for what seemed ages, I finally drew breath and waited. How would Stuart react? Would he be upset or angry? Would he stop being friends with me? Would he explain that such terrible behaviour meant that I could no longer be part of the church? Would **he** call me a hypocrite? All these questions flashed through my mind as I sat, hardly daring to look at his face, waiting for him to say something. All around me, groups of people were praying, not realising that my whole future hung in the balance.

Stuart was smiling. 'No need to look so worried!' he said. 'I forgive you.'

I waited, expecting at the least, an expression of disappointment or anger. There was nothing.

'What? Is that it?' I asked, almost indignantly.

'Well, yes, basically,' Stuart replied. 'God's forgiveness is absolute, no questions asked, so mine should be too. He forgives you and gives you a fresh start from now.'

I stared at him in disbelief. 'You mean, I've been putting myself through all this grief for nothing?'

Stuart laughed. 'Looks like it! You should have said something ages ago and we could have helped. God never wants you to feel guilty for long. As soon as you do, go to him and he can deal with it.'

Was it really as simple as that? I had learnt a valuable lesson that day, and one that I wanted to put into practice as soon as possible. God forgave me for the crack and the deceit and the wrong thoughts and actions. With this revelation came a return of that wonderful, cleansing peace I had experienced the night I became a Christian. I realised that this forgiveness did not mean that it was OK to commit all sorts of wrongs as long as I came back to God at some point. I never wanted to feel that guilty again. No, the forgiveness was the opportunity to start again, with the power to help me do it.

Conscience had never been a problem to me before, but now, I needed to be right with God. I had a relationship with him, and if things weren't right between us, then I couldn't be happy until they were. I had grown up seeing religion as something dead, kept going by a collection of browbeaten people living by a set of impossible rules that they couldn't keep. Now, I was beginning to understand the truth of the verse in the Bible that says that the Holy Spirit writes God's laws on our hearts. My responses were from within, not externally imposed.

I felt as if I was floating on air. The certainty of God's love for me, and the knowledge that I could have a fresh start and God didn't even remember all that I had done wrong was incredibly liberating. I wondered how he would help me to overcome the problems I'd had before, so that I didn't make the same mistakes again. Stuart had prayed for me at the end of the meeting, and I believed that God would answer his prayer. But I was amazed at the speed of the answer.

Later the same day, Stuart rang me at home. 'Hi, Ian. I've got an idea to run past you.'

'Yes?' I answered, wondering whether it involved a lot of hard work.

'Yeah, well you know I've got my own house?'

'Mmm.' Was this a decorating request perhaps?

'I wondered whether you'd like to share it with me. I've got room and could do with a lodger, from a financial point of view if nothing else.'

I was stunned. I'd been to Stuart's house and liked it very much. I found it hard to believe that he was offering to share it with a druggie, even a soon-to-be ex-druggie. I panicked at this startling generosity.

'Look, Stu, I'm really bowled over. Can I have a bit of time to think it through?'

'Of course,' he said readily. 'Let me know whenever.'

'Er … I suppose the offer includes Ziggy?'

Stuart laughed. 'Of course. I wouldn't dream of asking you without him!'

'Cheers. I'll get back to you as soon as I can.'

I made excuses to myself for delaying an answer. Deep down, though, I knew I was stalling. Moving in with Stuart would be the huge life change I needed to escape the slavery of the drugs. It was a practical expression of the fresh start God had promised. I wanted that so badly, yet at the same time I was scared of all that it involved. I realised that this was my big chance. Moving in with someone from the church would be a support and a challenge. Was I up to it? Very briefly, the temptation to stay where I was, in the life I knew, flashed through my mind. I reached for the phone.

'Stuart? It's Ian. Thanks very much for the offer of a room in your house. If you think you can put up with us, I'd love to take you up on it.'

Stuart sounded genuinely delighted by my decision, and told me that he believed God had told him to make the offer. I was overwhelmed by the whole situation. What a way to live! If someone had told me a few months ago that I would be moving house because God had spoken to a few people, including me, about it, I would have laughed aloud and assumed they were stoned. But this was exactly what was happening, and I loved it!

Within a week, I had moved out of my filthy bedsit forever. No more 'poo sandwich' or screaming alcoholics. No more long evenings surrounded by the litter of loneliness. No more shooting up in feverish, shaking haste before slipping into unconsciousness. As I drove away in Stuart's car, I felt a huge wave of relief and exhilaration. I was leaving more than the bedsit behind; I was leaving old thought patterns and habits, destructive routines and behaviour.

It was like heaven after what I had been used to – bright bedroom, clean bathroom, food in the cupboard, washing machine, and a comfortable, warm living area. I was no longer confined to one cell-like room, but free to make myself at home in the whole house. It took me quite a while to adjust to such luxury, and I never took it for granted. Every morning, I would wake up feeling relaxed and positive, no longer needing to search for a high, but instead becoming aware of the joy of God's Spirit in me. I revelled in the daily walk to the bathroom, and the shower that worked. Every time I put on clean clothes I felt grateful. It was as if I had bought an entirely new wardrobe. I loved the way that I could invite people back to 'my place' and be a giver of hospitality as well as a receiver. I felt transformed, no longer held back from living the new life I had entered.

It was not all plain sailing, though. Almost immediately, unwelcome opportunities arose to test whether I really was different now that I was a Christian, or whether it was all a delusion. The area we lived in was almost as run down and unsafe as Chapeltown and it didn't take me long to realise that there was drug dealing going on in our very street. Quite often, we had people calling at our house by mistake, looking for the local dealer. It would have been so easy to give them some money and ask them to get something for me.

I also found I had to work very hard on my attitudes and reactions. Soon after I moved into Stuart's house, a large family also moved in a few doors down the street. The children soon made their presence felt, with shouting, swearing and spiteful pranks on the neighbours. My first encounter was when one of the boys started throwing money at our kitchen window. I was incensed. Did he know that I had been a beggar, well used to kids throwing coins at me? I rushed outside, picked up the coin and marched across the road. The boy's mother answered the door, and behind her stood their dad – a huge, biker type who looked as if he wouldn't stand any nonsense. I wondered about turning round there and then, but decided to stand my ground.

'I've, er, just come to return the money your son threw at our kitchen window.'

Biker looked at me and scowled. 'Can't be our boy. He hasn't got any money.'

'I know, it's all been thrown at our house.'

The man stared at me for a moment then said, 'Leave it with me. If it was him, I'll sort it.'

I left it with him, but the children's conduct did not improve over the next few weeks. Neighbours' bins were set on fire several times, and once we caught them trying to saw down someone's tree. Most people in the street, though distressed by the behaviour, seemed afraid to take any direct action. They would stand and watch, complaining bitterly among themselves, but would not try to stop them.

One day, while working in the house, I heard a huge commotion in the street outside. Looking out, I saw a large gang of about 20 young people all picking on one boy. He was getting quite badly hurt with kicks and punches and I decided that this couldn't go on. I waded into the middle of the fight to break it up, and to my amazement, saw the mother of the difficult boys right in the midst, egging them on. I shouted at them, and everyone paused to see who had joined them so energetically. This at least stopped the fight. The mother started yelling abuse at me, accusing me in very insulting terms of interfering. The victim had made himself scarce, and the gang was dispersing, so I decided to disappear as well.

'A fine example you're setting your lads!' was my parting shot as I stalked off. She swore viciously in reply.

I was worried that I was reacting just as I would have done in the old days, although I was a lot more restrained now. I knew that as Christians we didn't have to be doormats and should stand up for what's right. The problem was getting the balance between that and showing love and forgiveness. When the boys began throwing eggs at houses, I didn't even try to find the balance. Stuart went for the 'bless those who are persecuting you' policy, and actually went out just after the eggs had been thrown and gave the boys some chocolate coins we had in. I couldn't be that nice, and felt that he was letting them get away with unacceptable behaviour. The boys also seemed to have a problem in accepting such kindness; half the coins were thrown back at the house soon afterwards.

So, when I came home the following day and discovered that the windows of our house were yet again covered in eggs, I felt it was the last straw. Furious, I went to the fridge, grabbed an egg, stormed outside and lobbed it at the troublemakers' house. As soon as the egg had left my hand, I regretted my impulsive action. It didn't score a direct hit on the window, but struck the wall just above and dribbled down over the glass. I beat a hasty retreat, but had taken no more than three steps before I felt God speak to me very clearly, in the form of a persistent thought, telling me to go and apologise for what I had done.

I knew that I wouldn't feel at peace until I had obeyed this compulsion from God. I was scared of Biker, but I was even more in awe of God. I kept an eye on the house, and when I saw Biker working in his backyard on the car, I knew the time had come. With a sinking heart, I set off to speak to him. He didn't look particularly pleased to see me, but leaned on the car, waiting for me to speak.

'Yeah, well, I've come with a bit of an apology,' I said, feeling a fool. Biker frowned and I rushed on with my explanation. 'If you look at my house, you'll see that it's covered in eggs that your kids have been throwing. I'm afraid I lost my cool and threw one back. I'm sorry about that.'

Biker gazed at his house and spotted the egg stains smeared down the window. Surprisingly, he barked with laughter, 'I don't blame you, mate. I'd have done the same and a bit more in your place. If it **was** my kids, they'll be in trouble.'

I breathed a sigh of relief, and we began chatting about all sorts of things. It turned out that we had quite a bit in common – he'd been in prison, and had visited the Isle of Man for the TT Races. Amazingly, we seemed to get on well, and I was able to tell him how things had changed for me since my own stints in prison. Just as I was going, he said, 'I shouldn't worry too much about the kids and their mischief – we're moving very soon.'

I took a polite interest in where they were going, but inside I was sending up prayers of thanks! In the three weeks before they left, we had no further trouble.

In the midst of all these distractions, I was finally winning my battle against drugs. Being in a new environment certainly helped. I had to form different routines and ways of doing things. Having Stuart around helped as well, because he encouraged me when I was finding it difficult. Within four months, I had come off the methadone, to the astonishment of the drugs counsellor and the GP. Everyone was amazed at the speed of my progress, and I told anyone who would listen that it was God who had helped me. I got some funny looks and smiles, but I didn't care. I knew it was true, and that

I had everything I needed to be a totally 'recovered' rather than 'recovering' addict.

But even with all these positive benefits, I still struggled at times. It was worst when I was upset or depressed about something. There were a couple of times when I did give in to the temptation to resort to my old way of dealing with problems. It was too easy, on my way home from work, to stop a dealer and ask him for some heroin. But even though the effects of the drug were strong, I didn't get any pleasure from it. Even when I was under the influence, I knew that I had done wrong and wanted to put things right. I didn't sink into a muzzy stupor as I normally would; instead I was bothered by guilt and grief. I had to do something about it right away. I found Stuart with another friend in the living-room. He looked concerned when he saw me, and they both listened in silence as I told them what I had done. Even though I felt so uncomfortable and ashamed, I didn't doubt that they would still accept me and love me.

I was right. Stuart and John prayed with me for strength, and I asked God for forgiveness. I was devastated at what I had done. Afterwards, they told me that even if

I didn't feel forgiven, I was, because of God's promises to his people. Nevertheless, it still took me a few days to know deep inside that God still loved me and had put the whole thing behind him.

And even then, I did the same thing again, a few weeks later. This time, I was tempted with crack, again at a point when I was feeling low. And again, I realised almost immediately the enormity of what I had done. This time, I not only felt guilty towards God and my long-suffering friends, but also towards myself. The crack had used up £400 of my first savings ever. I couldn't believe I had spoilt everything in this stupid way. Feeling sick with myself, I went to Stuart, wondering whether this time he would say that enough was enough. But he continued to show superhuman patience and concern and yet again we prayed for forgiveness and a fresh start. It seemed unbelievable that I could come back to God, having blown it so many times, but I learnt that there is no end to his mercy, so long as we truly mean that we are sorry. Though these were painful and humbling experiences, they reinforced my relationship with God, and my appreciation of him as a father.

I was worried that I would continually be struggling with the temptation to take drugs, that I would always be 'recovering' but never 'recovered'. I didn't want to live like that. I had tasted a life of true freedom, and I didn't want it spoilt by shackles from the past. I prayed that I would be completely free from the grip of drugs, and God answered my prayer in a most amazing way.

Stuart and I had become involved with Phil, a drug addict with a lot of problems. We had spent a great deal of time with him, trying to help him in any way we could. One evening, we received a phone call to say that he had overdosed and was dangerously ill. We dashed across to his flat, and saw that the ambulance had arrived. We agreed that Stuart should go down to the hospital with Phil while I got a few of his things together in a case to be brought down afterwards.

I went into the flat. It was a total mess, with clothes, dirty plates and half-eaten food all over the floor. I stooped to pick up some clothes, and as I did so, I noticed lots of tablets scattered across the room. They were the same ones that I had broken into the chemist's shop for all those years ago. Almost £800 worth of stuff lay at my feet, mine for the taking if I wanted it. And I **didn't** want it!

I looked at the tablets and felt a rush of joy. I really had no wish to take them. My relationship with God and the life I was now enjoying were far too valuable to risk for some short-term excitement. The attraction had completely gone.

Slowly, I picked up the tablets and put every single one of them carefully back in the container. I didn't have any feelings of regret or desire, just triumph and thankfulness. I was truly free of drugs; a recovered addict at last.

CHAPTER NINE

All change!

'I want to go back to the Isle of Man.'

Stuart looked up from his book, a bit surprised at this sudden statement. I had a book in front of me too, but I wasn't reading, just gazing into space. I had been thinking for a long time about my family. Now that life was so good for me, and I could think straight again after so many drug-befuddled years, I wanted to see them again. I realised that they had suffered a lot because of me, and I wanted to put things right if I possibly could. Stuart listened to me with a slight look of concern. I picked up on it.

'Why're you looking like that? I thought you'd be pleased.'

'Yeah, of course I am. It's really important to put things right. There's a lot of hurt on both sides, I know. I'm just a bit worried about how you'll cope when you go back to your old haunts. You might find it more difficult to resist temptation there. Especially if things go a bit pear-shaped with your family.'

He had a fair point, although I was a bit indignant that he thought I was so weak in my faith. Then I remembered the number of times he had stood by me when I had slipped into drug-taking again.

'I can see what you're saying, but I haven't even wanted to use since the night we took Phil to hospital. I'm sure I'll be OK.'

Nevertheless, when another friend, Richard, made the offer to come with me to the island, I was quite relieved to accept.

Now that the decision was made, I was alternately excited and very nervous. I sent my Gran a postcard to say I was coming. It was the first communication I'd had with her in over two years. I wondered how she would react to it. I also hoped that she would let my Dad and brother, Joey, know that the prodigal was returning.

Richard and I decided to camp for the three days we were there. I didn't feel I could ask my Gran if we could stay there, and we didn't want to spend money on Bed and Breakfast. As we approached the house, I felt more and more apprehensive. Just as we got there, I saw Gran and Grandad walking towards the door.

'Gran!' I yelled. 'It's me!'

She turned, and her face broke into a huge smile. 'Ian! Oh Ian! I thought you were dead.' She held me in an enormous hug. When she drew back, I saw there were tears in her eyes. Grandad, meanwhile, looked a bit awkward. He greeted me gruffly, and led the way into the house. Gran told me that until she had received my card the previous week, she had thought I was dead. She had prayed for me every night since I had left the island, and was overjoyed to see me again. I said how sorry I was that I had caused her such worry, and went on to tell her how I had become a Christian. Grandad seemed unmoved by the whole situation, and not very interested in what had been happening to me. I didn't care. It was enough that Gran was so delighted to see me, and that she so evidently forgave me for all the pain I had caused.

I decided to give my brother a ring and ask if he would like to meet up for a drink. He sounded very cool on the phone, and suspicious as to why I had come back. Eventually, he said that he was going out to a friend's that evening and might pass the pub where I said I would be. I didn't hold out much hope, but to my surprise, as I was sitting in the pub with Richard, Joey walked in. I was delighted to see him, but it obviously wasn't mutual. I bought him a drink, and tried to tell him how much I had changed, but he didn't seem convinced. Our conversation was stilted, with awkward pauses, and after one drink, he left. I was upset by this response, though I suppose I couldn't really blame Joey for thinking the worst of me.

It was very similar when I went to see my Dad and Joan. The last time I had seen them, I had defrauded them of £50, pretending that it was to pay my rent. Not surprisingly, therefore, they thought that my return to the island must be another money-acquiring exercise. It was a very uncomfortable meeting. Dad had been expecting a policeman at the door for the last two years to tell him I was dead. We were all experiencing a strange mix of emotions – relief, anger, pain, and a certain amount of happiness. None of us really knew what to say and how to relate to one another. I told them that I was a Christian, but I could see that this didn't move them either. They probably thought it was another ploy to get money out of them.

I felt very shaken after I had said goodbye to Dad and Joan. I had hoped for a much warmer reception, forgetting that they hadn't changed as much as I had. So much had happened to me in the intervening years, whereas the people here were pretty much as they were when I left. Their memories of me were not positive. Time had not healed the wounds I had inflicted.

Richard and I went for a walk in the surrounding countryside, and I was glad of his companionship and encouragement. As we strolled along, enjoying Ziggy's mad antics, I noticed a group of people coming towards us. As they drew nearer, I realised with a jolt that Jess was there. My hands grew clammy and my heart rate speeded up alarmingly. She was with her parents, her sister and a man I didn't recognise. As they passed, I saw the shock of recognition in her eyes. She lifted her hand and looked as if she was going to say something. Her father, though, with a curt nod and set face, strode on, drawing the group with him. I had only had time to smile at her in greeting.

I stood and stared at the receding figures. Of all the people to meet, on my first brief visit to the Isle of Man, Jess was the least likely. It was a very, very long time since I had seen her, but she still had such an effect on me. If only she hadn't been with the others.

Richard listened sympathetically as I explained who she was and how I felt. We carried on, and came out near an old drug den. I pointed it out to Richard, and as I was telling him about it, I saw that Ronnie, one of my old mates, was there. We went over to say hello. I was still stunned from having seen Jess, so it felt even stranger to see another face from my past. We chatted for a bit and I told him that I was clean from drugs. He found this incredible, knowing how I had been before. He listened politely to my explanation about becoming a Christian.

'Good on ya mate,' was his response. 'If it works for you, go for it.' This wasn't quite the reaction I was looking for, but at least I had tried. 'And another thing, Ian,' he said, winking at Richard, 'it's a good thing you brought a minder along. I mean, I wouldn't have **offered** you any stuff, like, but I know what you're like at persuading me!'

We laughed, but I knew he had a point. I had become so upset after my meetings with Dad and Joey, and then the chance encounter with Jess. It would have been so simple to relapse into past habits, and make myself feel better with a shot of heroin, slipping back so easily into familiar territory.

'Yeah, thanks Rich, for coming with me,' I said. He smiled, but I knew he understood exactly what I meant.

We left the Isle of Man the following day, and I felt a bit frustrated. I had so wanted to see my family relationships restored, and not a lot seemed to have been achieved. I suppose I had been a bit naive not to have understood that fragile relationships take a long time to mend. I was particularly bothered by Joey's reaction. We had not been brought up together for very long, and he'd had a difficult childhood, in and out of the Children's Home. But I still felt a bond with him, and had fond memories of my baby brother. We had lost touch with each other as we had grown up, although we had occasionally met by chance. He obviously had heard of some of my more notorious exploits.

At Christmas, I sent my family cards and gifts. In Joey's card, I wrote about God's forgiveness, and suggested he take a leaf out of God's book. Maybe it was not the most tactful of Christmas greetings, but I wrote as I felt. I wanted to return to the island to see the family again, and longed for him to be pleased to see me.

One weekend, when I was at a Christian conference in Wales, I met a couple from Australia. They had come all the way to Britain because they believed that God was calling them to return to the place of the wife's birth. They had initially believed that to be England, but during the weekend, they discovered that she originally came from the Isle of Man. They planned to go there almost immediately, and stay for quite some time. They extended an open invitation to me to come and stay with them whenever I was on the island. I was overwhelmed, both by the way that God had provided an answer to a practical need of mine, and also how, in the Christian family, you have relatives everywhere, who are willing to do anything for you.

Now that I had a base on the island, I decided to go back at Easter. It was great to see my Australian friends again, and we had a good time. I believed that God had told me not to get in touch with Joey this time, but leave him to make the first move. I found it really difficult to stick to this. Every time I drove past his flat, I was so tempted to call in. But something held me back. I did see Dad and Joan a few times, and the relationship was much improved. We were far more relaxed and Dad began to see that the change in me was real. I was obviously much more healthy and fit than when he had last seen me, and my whole attitude was different. What confirmed the change for him though, was when he offered me some money as I was going, and I didn't accept it. He was astonished, as I had never been known to refuse money before!

This weekend had been far more positive than the previous one, and I felt encouraged that relations with Gran, Dad, Joan and even Grandad were being restored. My one disappointment was about Joey, but I still felt that I should not contact him. I returned to Leeds, only to receive a phone message via the church office from Joey. He said that he had heard I was on the island and was sorry to have missed me. Could I ring him back? I was delighted, and rang back almost immediately. We had a great conversation and I felt that we were brothers again. It was a valuable lesson about being obedient to God, even when it went against my natural way of doing things.

My relationship with Joey was sealed a year or so later. I had kept in touch with my family and visited the Isle of Man as often as I could. Each time, some progress was made in repairing the damage of years. Then, when I needed a holiday, it occurred to me that Joey might like to go with me. I rang him up and at first he dithered. He was married by then, and about to become a father. His wife, though, pointed out that this was probably the last time he would be able to take time off in this way. With her blessing, he agreed, and we set off to Tenerife.

It was a golden time. All the reserve and barriers that had grown up over the years were demolished and we got to know each other properly as brothers again. Symbolically, perhaps, a significant point was when, having had a few drinks on the first night, we decided to go skinny-dipping on the deserted beach. We stripped off our clothes and raced into the moonlit water, laughing like little children again. It was only as we emerged to loud cheers that we realised that we were in full view of a nearby bar and had attracted quite a large audience. In the midst of the hilarious embarrassment of the incident, we really bonded that night and had a wonderful week.

Another high point – literally and figuratively – was a trip we made by cable-car to the top of a volcano. The views were breathtaking and we both felt overawed by the amazing creation we could see stretched out beneath us. It was a defining moment for us both. We discovered that we were very similar and understood each other surprisingly well. We returned home from that holiday refreshed physically and mentally, but also closer than we had ever been before.

My grandfather had always been a frightening figure in my life. As a child I had steered clear of him whenever possible, and as teenager, I had resented and defied him. I had always used my Gran as a shield from him and she

had mediated constantly between us all the time I had
lived with them. Our terrible rows had never been
resolved, just left until time buried them. Now that I was
a Christian, I wanted all my relationships to be right,
including my relationship with Grandad. Every time I
went to see him and Gran, he was polite but not friendly.
It was difficult to get through to him. I also realised that I
still felt very hurt and rejected by him, and tended to try
and ignore the whole issue, concentrating instead on
other members of the family. One day, however, I had a
phone call from Gran. She sounded upset.

'It's your Grandad,' she said. 'He's ill.'

'Has he been to the doctor?'

'Yes, lots of times. They couldn't work out what
the problem was, so they sent him for tests. Oh, Ian,
it's cancer.'

I was shocked. My grandfather was such a proud
man. I couldn't imagine him being defeated by such a vile
disease. I promised to come over as soon as I could.

When I walked into the bedroom, I could hardly
believe this was the same man. Grandad had always been
large and physically strong. He was a huge presence in the

house with his big frame and loud voice. Now, he was small and gaunt, a shrivelled shadow of his former self. He was obviously dying. I was so distressed by the change in him that I couldn't stop myself giving way to tears as I greeted him. I quickly left the room so as not to upset Gran and Grandad with my show of emotion, and stood in the living-room, looking out of the window but unable to see a thing because my eyes were blinded with tears. As I wept, I prayed for my grandparents, and also asked forgiveness for the bitterness and anger I had harboured towards Grandad all these years. Because I was so skilful at repressing my feelings, I hadn't even realised how strongly I felt against Grandad until forced to face up to his illness and impending death. As I prayed, a familiar peace filled me. At last, I had forgiven my grandfather.

He had been bedridden for the past three weeks, and had passed a great deal of blood. Over the next two weeks of my stay, though, he improved significantly, and could get up and move around. We drew a lot closer in this time, and I was able to talk to him quite openly about what Jesus had done for me, and could do for him.

With the imminence of death, Grandad had lost all the pride that had made him so hard and distant. He listened to all that I told him and seemed to accept the truth of it. Our relationship was whole at last, and I was so thankful. Gran, too, was really delighted that I was there and that we were getting on so well.

As Grandad was making such good progress, I decided that I had better return to Leeds. No sooner had I got back there, though, than I received a phone call telling me that he had taken a turn for the worse. By the time I arrived in the Isle of Man again, Grandad was in hospital and was heavily sedated, unable to recognise anyone. As he lay there, hovering between life and death, I thought about all the pain and damage he had caused me over the years, and then thought about the past few weeks. I was very, very glad that God had given me the opportunity to put things right.

Someone had come into the hospital room. It was Joey, tears in his eyes. He hadn't seen Grandad for 25 years. I could only guess at the emotions he was feeling.

'I'm so glad you came,' I said in a low voice.

'I had to,' he said simply. 'He's still my Grandad.'

I returned to Leeds after the funeral, emotionally drained, yet also feeling at peace with my family and myself.

At the same time as all my efforts to repair relationships, I was also making changes in my working life. I had been selling the Big Issue for many years, several of them since becoming a Christian, and felt it was time I moved on. I had signed off from the dole, to the astonishment of the staff there. One of them actually saw me afterwards, and asked why I had signed off. I explained that I was making too much selling the Big Issue to qualify for the dole. She suggested that I should sign on anyway. When I said that I felt that was dishonest, and that as a Christian, I couldn't do it, she was amazed, and was a little uncomfortable with my attitude.

I had told all the Big Issue vendors that I had become a Christian, and over the years, they had seen for themselves the changes in me. The most obvious was that I no longer used drugs, and was much happier and healthier than I had ever been. Whereas before, I had been morose and depressed, now I was genuinely cheerful and optimistic. Another noticeable difference was my language. Before, every second word of mine had been a four-letter one, but I found that being around people who didn't swear made it seem really out of place. Although very occasionally I slipped up, generally I had dropped swear words completely from my vocabulary.

The guys on the street would also have seen a change in my ability to handle myself. I used to get angry really quickly and couldn't cope very well in challenging situations. Since I had become a Christian, however, I was able to hold on to my temper much more effectively. For one thing, situations didn't bother me as much as they once had, and I also had the power of the Holy Spirit to help me control my anger.

This difference in me was demonstrated plainly one Christmas when the vendors had got together in a local pub for a Christmas party. I was excited about Christmas for the first time since being a small child. It had real meaning for me this time. I was keen to tell the people I worked with, many of whom had the same problems that I'd had, about the joy and peace I had found in becoming a Christian. I spotted Bill, one of the guys working in the centre of Leeds, propped against the bar on his own. He was built like the side of a house, and had a reputation for being a bit of a bully. Just the sort of person, I reasoned, who most needed to hear what I had to say. I wandered over and propped myself up next to him. He didn't seem that pleased to see me. It was quickly evident that he had been drinking for some time. I started chatting, telling him all that had been happening to me. At first, he seemed quite interested, but then, as I mentioned God a few times, he got a bit uncomfortable and told me to shut up. I shifted my attention to another bloke who happened to be standing next to Bill, and who had been listening as well. Grinning at him, I continued my story, telling him about my experiences when I was filled with the Holy Spirit. Bill's face grew redder and redder and he clenched his fist.

'I told you to shut it!' he burst out. 'You're doing my head in. Now shut your gob or I'll shut it for you.'

Normally, this sort of situation would have lit my short fuse very quickly. I wasn't a violent character, but I didn't like being threatened, and could lose my temper rapidly. Now, though, I felt peaceful and in control.

'It's OK, mate. God loves you – and so do I.'

Bill was at exploding point. 'I'm gonna take you outside and kick your head in!' he roared.

'It wouldn't make any difference to the fact that God loves you, and so do I.'

The whole pub had gone quiet, and many people were looking curiously at me, wondering why I hadn't reacted. Bill looked as if steam was coming out of his ears.

'You b***** little twat. I'm gonna glass your face and that'll stop you. C'mon outside, you f*****.'

I stood my ground and kept calm. 'God would still love you – and so would I.'

He exploded with a loud yell and lunged towards me, punching me hard on the nose. I reeled back but managed to stay standing.

'God still loves you, and so do I,' I said, slightly muffled by the blood pouring out of my nose.

Bill practically melted with embarrassment. He took one look at everyone clustered round, shook his head and slunk off to a far corner of the pub, where he stayed for about ten minutes before leaving.

I was surrounded by a mob of people all congratulating me on my performance. I had just been punched on the nose, but it felt as if I had defeated a world champion. One of the staff in the pub said that he had never seen anything like it in his life. Despite the discomfort and the blood, I felt on top of the world.

When I finally decided to stop working for the Big Issue, I thought that I would like to throw a big party to thank all the people who had supported me over the years. I had many loyal customers, some of whom I had not always treated that well in the past. I wanted to show them how much I appreciated them. The idea, which first came to me when I was listening to a sermon, took hold and I couldn't let it go. I had never organised any type of event at all, let alone one on this scale, so the prospect was a bit daunting.

As might be expected, I didn't have any money for this venture. I had actually managed to save some, but had already spent it on a car, before having the idea, so had none to spare. I was determined not to ask people to help financially, but instead, prayed about it and went ahead anyway. Many of my friends at church offered to help practically, which was great. Then, one day, someone came to me and gave me £500 specifically towards the party. I was astounded. I had never asked for money, nor hinted that it was a problem. This could only have been God. In the following weeks, I received various generous gifts, until I had an amazing £2,000 at my disposal.

I thought that using the church building for the party might put some people off, so began looking for a convenient city centre venue. Finding one, though, proved to be quite a problem. Many venues refused because they didn't want the potential nuisance of lots of homeless people on their premises. Others demanded a £1,000 deposit, which was out of the question, while still more were booked up because it was the Christmas party season. Eventually, I found somewhere that would take us at a reasonable rate. Unbelievably, two weeks before the party date, they pulled out, leaving the party as homeless as some of the guests.

The thought flashed through my mind that perhaps I should call the whole thing off. After all, it wasn't my fault that there was no venue. Everyone would appreciate the gesture, and at least this way, the party couldn't be a flop. But I knew there was no way I was going to stop now. I didn't even panic, because

I knew God would not let me down. It was his idea in the first place.

I was discussing the problem with one of my customers when she was suddenly struck with inspiration. She took me to meet a friend of hers who was manager of Browns, a city centre bar. Incredibly, he not only agreed to let us hold the party there, but also let us have it for nothing, and offered to put on extra bar staff for the evening. I was overwhelmed!

Safeway, the backdrop of my enterprises for so many years, agreed to do the catering, and generously gave me a discount. I even managed to find a professional entertainer, via Cannon and Ball's agent. The invitations took a massive seven hours to put together on the computer, as I was somewhat technologically challenged, but were finally completed and looked brilliant. Somehow, the media had heard of the project, and various newspaper, radio and television companies expressed an interest in coming along. Prior to that, they even came along to film Ziggy and me selling the Big Issue. All this positive attention was quite mind-blowing for someone whose previous public and media appearances had only been in court.

Everything was in place, and as the day of the party dawned, I realised that I was extremely nervous. I pictured a 'worst case scenario', which was me dying as I stood up to speak. But death held no fears for me now that I knew where I was going, so even the worst was not so bad! Having persuaded myself out of my nerves, I set off. By the time I arrived, with a freshly bathed Ziggy, my helpers from the church were hard at work. The place looked fantastic, with streamers and balloons, beautifully decorated tables, and all the food set out in a tantalising array.

Everyone came and it was obvious they were all having a wonderful time. The television crew mingled and ate with the rest, filming and interviewing the whole time. It certainly increased the glamour of the event.

Finally, the moment came that I had been dreading. I stood up in front of two hundred guests and a camera crew and started to speak. I simply told the story of how I had reached this point, and how I so desperately wanted them to experience the same life change that I'd had, and come to know the real meaning of Christmas. Halfway through, a local shopkeeper who was a little the worse for drink heckled me. At first, I made the mistake of being drawn into debate with her, but then she was quietened by one of the helpers, and I managed to regain my composure and the thread of my speech.

When I had finished, I sank down in relief, knowing that I'd said what I'd needed to – and I hadn't died. To my amazement, people were on their feet, cheering wildly and stamping on the floor in approval. The rest of the evening was like a dream. I was surrounded by a crowd of people all wanting to ask questions or make comments. It was such a marvellous opportunity to share with them how great life had been since I had become a Christian. When it was finally all over, and the guests had gone away happy, I went home and enjoyed the best night's sleep since I'd begun this project.

I still had three weeks to go before finishing with the Big Issue, so the next day, I went to my pitch as usual, and was amazed at how many people stopped me to comment on the party. Everyone was really positive, and I realised that the significance of that night had rippled out far beyond those who were actually present. The other Big Issue vendors and homeless people were very pleased because for once they had been portrayed in a positive light. I was the lead story in every news bulletin and had my picture on the front of several newspapers. I remembered the last time I had received press attention – when I was sentenced for breaking into the chemist's shop – and felt so grateful that my life had turned round so totally since then. I wasn't going to let all the fame go to my head, though. I'd had too much experience of pride – my own and others' – to let it get a hold at this point.

When I finally finished selling the Big Issue, I felt a mixture of sadness and excitement. It had been a lifeline to me, and since I had become a Christian, it had also been a means of meeting a much wider cross-section of society than I would ever normally expect to. But I was also excited at what the future held. I didn't actually have a job to go to, but just believed that God was telling me it was time to move on. My unemployment continued for a couple of months, but I was not fazed by this. I didn't sign on, because I wanted to rely totally on God, and spent my time helping out people in the church. Then one day, a friend mentioned that I should apply to work at St George's Crypt, one of the main homeless shelters in

Leeds. I pointed out that no job had been advertised for me to apply for, but my friend said that if I wrote to them, I was sure to get an interview. He was right, and to make matters even simpler for me, a member of staff at the Crypt told me his predictions as to the interview questions. Sure enough, these came up almost immediately, making me chuckle. The interviewers asked me what was amusing, so I told them that I knew what to expect. The interview took off from that point with everyone relaxing, creating a much more informal atmosphere. I ended up telling them how I had come to be in this position, and although they said they would let me know, I was sure of the outcome of the interview before I ever left the room.

I spent a year working for the Crypt, and it certainly was full of challenges and even conflict at times. Because I had been on 'the other side', I understood only too well what some of our clients were going through, and this made it hard to be detached. Also, I knew the majority of them personally, and found it difficult at first to be in a position of authority over them. They thought that I would do them special favours since I was one of them, while I only longed for them to come into all the freedom and peace that I had experienced. They didn't always appreciate my motives, having hoped that my understanding would lead to a bit of leniency.

Adjusting to my new role was certainly a challenge. It seemed very strange to be in such close contact with drugs and users and yet not be using myself. It was exciting to go in every day and not be tempted. I could so easily have slipped back into my old ways with so much exposure to the drug culture, but I never had the slightest desire. I could see all too clearly now the horrific damage that drugs do to individuals and society, and I was dedicated to fighting them.

Obviously, drugs were not tolerated at all at the Crypt, and a positive asset to my role there was that my intimate knowledge of the drugs scene meant that I was able to detect very early when they were being used. I recognised the different ways people tried to get round the ban – I had tried them all myself at various times. So, I used to go into the toilets and shout over the tops of the cubicles to people who were shooting up, telling them that they had better stop or get out. I could see when someone had just injected and would gently but firmly escort them out. Once, I realised that someone was dealing in the building. I took him to one side and explained that his activities would get the place closed down, thus damaging the very people he lived and worked with. He appeared to appreciate my approach and respect me for it, and quietly left the premises.

I often had to deal one-to-one with clients, which I enjoyed. Part of the job was arranging accommodation for homeless people. I had to interview them and then ring round all the various possibilities on their behalf. It was great when I managed to arrange something for them and send them on to their new accommodation. Sometimes, however, interviews were not always fruitful.

People often needed someone to talk to, and I was happy to be a listening ear and offer what help I could. But when a young girl came to talk to me, very upset and wanting to talk about relationship problems and sexual matters, I realised that I was out of my depth. Not only that, but I risked compromising my own position. She was in such an emotional state that anything I said or did might be misinterpreted. I left the room as soon as I could and found someone more appropriate to help her. Then I went to see my boss to say that I never wanted to be put in such a situation again.

Another aspect of my job was working in the various hostels in the city. I would spend some time doing administrative work and some time supervising the residents. They were certainly an interesting mix of people; some from suprisingly unexpected backgrounds who had lost everything through drink or drugs.

One older chap was evidently something of an artist, and many of his paintings were hung around the hostel. One evening when I was on duty, a group of men were watching an innocuous television programme about animals' achievements. Suddenly there was uproar. Joe, the artist, was raging around the place, shouting and swearing, and telling anyone who would listen that he was the only artist and he wasn't going to put up with anyone else trying to be one. I was mystified until I caught a glimpse of the television. A picture of an elephant wielding a paintbrush filled the screen. It took about 20 minutes to calm Joe down. This made me realise again how very insecure and vulnerable these apparently tough guys are.

Back at the Crypt I used various tactics to persuade clients to go to the daily Chapel service. My most successful was to play table tennis against them, with the agreement that the loser would go to Chapel. What people didn't realise until too late was that I was an ace table tennis player. My Grandad had taught me all those years ago, and then, when I was in prison, I perfected my technique to the extent that I always had to have a handicap. As a result, quite a few homeless people made their way a bit shamefacedly to the Chapel over the year. All I wanted in my work at the Crypt, was to help people get out of the misery of their situation and find true peace and fulfilment as I had.

One of the triumphs of the job was the trust put in me by others – and the fact that I never betrayed that trust. One weekend, I was even left in sole charge of a hostel, where I had to ensure everything was running smoothly and also hand out spending money and medication to the residents. The fact that I, one time thief and user of the very drugs I was now handing out, could be given such a responsibility was fantastic. The change in my life was real and permanent, and obvious to others as well as to myself.

CHAPTER TEN
Postscript

I watched the young man as he twitched his way down the middle of the street. He kept squatting down and then jerking up violently, as if someone was pulling at invisible strings, attached to his arms and trunk. His face was like a mask, and his vacant eyes gazed unseeingly at the busy shoppers swerving to avoid him. Inside his head, he may have been experiencing all sorts of weird sensations, but from the outside, I could see him for what he was; a sick, damaged, pitiful human, controlled by an evil force which would ultimately destroy him.

For so many years, I too had been manipulated by the deadly puppeteer, my life moving to his command, until I had been set free and the invisible strings cut for good. As I observed this youth, out of his head on drugs, my heart ached for him and the thousands like him. I dedicated myself, with God's help, to fighting the evil of addiction and its roots and to showing people a new life offered through Jesus. I knew too, that there were so many more who were not such obvious 'puppets on a string'. They might not be addicted to drugs or alcohol or crime, yet they were still controlled by selfishness and wrongdoing, or weighed down by pain and misery. I wanted to be able to show them, too, God's love and power.

Since becoming a Christian, I have proved more and more the reality of my faith. It is not based on empty words peddled by self-righteous hypocrites. Nor have I become a religious nutter. I simply have a relationship with my Creator, who is also my Father. This relationship affects my whole life; my attitudes, my lifestyle, my friendships, my character and my decisions. And because I know forgiveness in my own life, I have been able to forgive those who wronged me in the past.

I have not returned to my drug-taking habits, as so many of my friends – and the experts – thought I would. Instead, for quite some time now, I have been working for the church, raising Christ's profile in the city, and reaching out to the needy in whatever way I can.

Much of my work involves going into schools, either to take assemblies or to be part of RE or PSHCE lessons. I often take Ziggy with me, and begin my talk by pretending that he is a sniffer dog specially trained to detect cigarettes. This usually creates a ripple of interest and, in some cases, concern. I build up the drama for a while and when I say that I am going to let him off the lead so that he can come amongst the pupils to do his job, I (and probably the teachers!) can immediately tell the children who have cigarettes hidden on them. Only at the last moment do I tell them that the dog is not really going to sniff out the culprits. As they relax, I go on to tell them that I have more than once been at the mercy of a sniffer dog – and why. The introduction never fails to grab and keep their attention, and the response from young people in schools has been amazing.

I have also worked on short-term projects in other places, sometimes abroad, but mostly in this country. I spent three weeks in a seaside town in Wales, helping support the work of a church there. Some amazing things happened, which could only be down to God.

I was at one meeting and there was a group of girls at the back who were messing about, talking and laughing quite loudly when someone was speaking. I felt really frustrated, because I knew that what was being said could transform their lives. Eventually, I went outside to calm down, and as I was there, God spoke to me really clearly about something that had happened to one of the girls. It was sensitive, and I didn't want to embarrass her, so I went back in and asked if I could have a word with her. She didn't seem to react at all to what I said, and I wondered whether I had got it wrong. Then, she left the meeting, followed by one of her friends. They both returned quite soon, and the friend told me that the girl was really shaken. Apparently, I had told her something true about her own life that she had not even told her best friend. I went to chat to her, explaining that God only works like that for a reason, to show her that he's there for her. At the end of the meeting, she and two of her friends became Christians.

Over the next few nights, another 20 of that group of girls became Christians. It was a wonderful experience and not surprisingly, increased my own faith and confidence.

In all this time, my relationship with God has grown stronger. Life is not perfect, of course; I have my ups and downs the same as anyone else. There are times when things go wrong and times when I feel upset and depressed. I learnt early on that being a Christian does not protect you from difficulties and challenges. The difference is that now I have an inner strength from God to deal with them. Knowing him means that I have a completely changed perspective on events and circumstances. And I receive guidance as to what I should do, and insight into various situations – my own and other people's. It's an exciting way to live! Best of all is the security that comes from being loved totally and unconditionally by someone who is committed and able to change me.

Many times, I think back to that day on the beach as a child, when I listened to the man with the easel. That was the beginning of learning about God's plan for mankind – and how very glad I am that now I know the full story! Without it, none of us can fulfil our true destiny. The story goes like this:

God made a perfect world, and created humans to live and rule in it as his friends. However, they made the choice to disobey him, and, as soon as they did, sin entered the world and caused a separation between man and God. God could no longer be intimate with them because his love is so pure and holy that it cannot allow anything which is not pure and holy near it. This then was the beginning of wrongdoing, pain, injustice and disease in our world and they spread like cancer, across the globe and over the millennia.

God was grief-stricken by this separation which was not of his making. He didn't want anyone to spend eternity without him. He wanted to get mankind out of the mess it had made for itself, but only someone not affected by sin could fight it. Jesus, his son, was that person, because he was totally without sin. He was conceived supernaturally, born to Mary, and lived a perfect life, full of power and love. His radical approach and profound relationship with his Father proved too much of a threat to the religious authorities of the day, and they had him put to death by crucifixion.

In that agonising death, Jesus paid the ultimate price on mankind's behalf. He, who was perfect in every way, was punished for each vile, evil, selfish action or thought that had happened in the past or would happen in the future. He, who was part of the Father, was cut off from him. It was unimaginable hell. But, because he was pure, and did not deserve the punishment, he was able to deal with it once and for all. Death and hell was the sentence that Jesus served, but because he was perfect, he only had to serve it for a short while. The power of God's love and goodness was even greater than death, and after three days, he rose to life again. The Evil One was defeated because he had no hold on Jesus, and Jesus was paying for all the people he **did** have a hold on. Now, it was possible for ordinary people to have a proper relationship with God again, just as Adam and Eve did, because Jesus had created a bridge of forgiveness to walk over. The access to God was via Jesus, because he had paid the price for our wrong doing and thinking. And once we take the opportunity offered to us, to have a relationship with God and Jesus, our lives are transformed into how they were originally intended to be.

My whole purpose in life is to make people aware of this wonderful story and its significance for them. That's not to say that I have become an intense 'Bible basher', preaching at anyone who will listen. I live life to the full and have great fun, always aware of the guiding presence of God's Holy Spirit, and his law 'written in my heart'. I don't live under lots of rules and regulations, but instead, enjoy a freedom I never thought possible. I can go into a pub and have a drink and never feel the need or desire to get drunk. I can pass dealers on the street and have not the slightest wish to experience again the adrenalin rush of a fix.

As I buy my copy of the Big Issue, I know that the biggest issue anyone will have to face in life, and at death, is where they stand with God. Tackling and resolving the biggest issue has been my salvation, my transformation and my joy.

The last word?

Maybe you have felt God tugging at your heart strings while reading this book, and maybe you have recognised your need to get right with God. There follows a short prayer which you may want to pray and if so, it needs to be done from the bottom of your heart:

Lord Jesus, I am sorry for all the things that I have done wrong in my life. Please forgive me and help me to turn from everything that I know is wrong. Thank you that you died for me personally so that I could be forgiven and have a new beginning. Thank you for that forgiveness and for your Holy Spirit. I give my life to you. Please come into my life, be the boss and be with me forever. Amen.

All you need to do now is find a lively local church and tell somebody what you have done. If you are unsure of where to go, I would be happy to point you in the right direction.

I can be contacted by writing to:

City Church Leeds

Ashwood Hall

44a Headingley Lane

Leeds

LS6 2EB

For specific help with drug-related issues I recommend that you contact the following Christian rehab centre:

Betel – (01564) 822356